Nietzsche in China

Literature and the Sciences of Man

Peter Heller
General Editor

Vol. 11

PETER LANG
New York • Washington, D.C./Baltimore • Boston
Bern • Frankfurt am Main • Berlin • Vienna • Paris

Shao Lixin

Nietzsche in China

PETER LANG
New York • Washington, D.C./Baltimore • Boston
Bern • Frankfurt am Main • Berlin • Vienna • Paris

Library of Congress Cataloging-in-Publication Data

Shao, Lixin
Nietzsche in China / Shao Lixin.
p. cm. — (Literature and the sciences of man; vol. 11)
Includes bibliographical references and index.
1. Philosophy, Chinese—20th century. 2. China—Intellectual life—20th century.
3. Nietzsche, Friedrich Wilhelm, 1844–1900. 4. China—Civilization—Western
influences. I. Title. II. Series.
B5231.S525   181'.11—dc21   98-26798
ISBN 0-8204-2853-1
ISSN 1040-7928

Die Deutsche Bibliothek-CIP-Einheitsaufnahme

Shao, Lixin:
Nietzsche in China / Shao Lixin.
–New York; Washington, D.C./Baltimore; Boston; Bern;
Frankfurt am Main; Berlin; Vienna; Paris: Lang.
(Literature and the sciences of man; Vol. 11)
ISBN 0-8204-2853-1

The paper in this book meets the guidelines for permanence and durability
of the Committee on Production Guidelines for Book Longevity
of the Council of Library Resources.

© 1999 Peter Lang Publishing, Inc., New York

All rights reserved.
Reprint or reproduction, even partially, in all forms such as microfilm,
xerography, microfiche, microcard, and offset strictly prohibited.

Printed in the United States of America

Acknowledgments

Over the past eight years this book, from a vague idea, to a dissertation, and to its current form, has served as a catalyst to radical changes in my views about modern Chinese history, and about history in general. As I am leaving the book to the public, my hearty gratitude goes to those who have sustained me with their wisdom and friendship.

I treasure the memory of the many editing sessions I have had with Professor Peter Heller who has not only instructed me on how to write better but also lent me what I dearly needed—self-confidence and the courage to continue. I am very grateful to Professor Wilma Iggers who twice read my drafts and whose insightful suggestions and criticism have improved this book to a great extent. I am only afraid that the final product, with its many errors for which I am solely responsible, will not bear out the enormous help I have received from them.

This book grew out of a dissertation which I wrote as a graduate student at the State University of New York at Buffalo. Professor Georg Iggers encouraged the project from the very beginning and his guidance and tolerance was crucial to its completion. In the stage of dissertation, I also received help from other faculty members. Professor Roger DesForges introduced me to important sources of Chinese history, read my drafts and gave me valuable advice. Professor Aleksander Gella read my dissertation and wrote encouraging comments. In my research on Chinese intellectuals, I am indebted to his perceptive studies of Polish intelligentsia. Professor Orville Murphy read the early drafts and kindly encouraged me to present my ideas at academic conferences.

Professor Bernice Glatzer Rosenthal of Fordham University has given me specific suggestions in regard to the book's contents and structure since 1991. Had she not called my attention to Nietzsche's influence on Mao Zedong, the book would have only seven chapters, instead of eight, as it now stands. Her own works on Russian and Soviet literature have always been a source of inspiration to me.

Professor June Grasso of Boston University has given me advice on source books and called my attention to many errors in the book's manuscript. I also want to take the opportunity to thank her for her book

Modernization and Revolution in China which has enlivened my Chinese history class since 1993 when I began to teach at the University of Minnesota Duluth.

Dr. Patricia Nultemeier read the book's final draft and made many valuable suggestions. I have benefited from her fine sense of the English language and appreciate her encouragement.

I want to thank my friends Zhang Dongdong and Wang Hongyan from the Australian National University, and Wong Laifan from the Northwestern University for Chinese sources they found for me.

Special thanks go to Dawn Littleton who helped me in many ways with writing the dissertation and the book's early drafts. This book reminds me of her admirable character.

My brother Shao Xiaogang read the book's draft and made good suggestions. He created the template file which I have used to format the book.

Finally I would like to thank my parents Shao Lin and Zhai Xuemei for their enduring support.

Contents

Preface ix

A Note on the Transcription
of Chinese Proper Names xi

1   Liang Qichao: Nietzsche and Reverse Social Darwinism 1

2   Wang Guowei: A Nietzsche That Is Believable
    But Not Lovable 15

3   Nietzsche and the "New Culture" 29

4   Lu Xun: "A Nietzschean Man of Strength" 45

5   Mao Zedong's Nietzsche Complex 79

6   Li Shicen: Nietzsche versus Chinese Traditions 91

7   Chen Quan: the Appropriation of Nietzsche by the Right 101

8   Zhou Guoping: Nietzsche At the Turn of the Century 115

Selected Bibliography 135

Index 141

Preface

Those readers whose interest is mainly in Nietzsche's philosophy may be amused or bemused by some Chinese interpretations of Nietzsche presented in this book. With two or three exceptions, most Chinese figures studied here were drawn to Nietzsche for non-philosophical reasons and had never had a more than superficial knowledge of him. Their utterances about Nietzsche are not philosophical speculations but coded political or social messages understood only in their particular historical contexts.

Nietzsche in China is first of all an intellectual history of twentieth century China. For nearly a hundred years, some of the most influential scholars, writers, political activists, and theorists in China have been fascinated by the German philosopher. Their responses to him testify to the dramatic transformation of Chinese consciousness during the period. Nietzsche serves as a good pretext for writing the story of this transformation.

A modest goal of the book is to delineate the long journey the Chinese have made in learning Western ideas, from the starting point a hundred years ago where Chinese intellectuals were ignorant of basic Western philosophical categories to a point now where they are capable of participating in philosophical dialogues on Western terms. (The author by no means suggests that a philosophical dialogue has to be conducted exclusively on either Western or Eastern terms.)

Nietzsche in China is also a psychological-philosophical analysis of modern Chinese intellectuals. Readers will notice that certain chapters pay more attention to the psychological processes behind written words, while others carefully follow philosophical arguments. In all cases every historical figure is questioned relentlessly about the real motive and meaning of his remarks about Nietzsche. In addition to revealing the main contents of the Chinese consciousness in the twentieth century, the author tries to bring to light habits of thinking common to many Chinese intellectuals. It is Nietzsche's presence in China that has made such a collective intellectual biography possible.

A Note on the Transcription of Chinese Proper Names

In this book all Chinese proper names are transcribed in *Pinyin*, a system of phonetic romanization that was first adopted by the People's Republic of China in 1958 and is now used by the US government, the United Nations, and many scholarly publications. There are four exceptions: the place names of Hong Kong and Canton and the personal names of Sun Yat-sen and Chiang Kai-shek are kept in their more familiar forms.

All Chinese personal names are given in their original order, that is, the family name first and the given name last. To avoid confusing Western readers, the book refers to all Chinese figures always by their full names.

CHAPTER 1

Liang Qichao:

Nietzsche and Reverse Social Darwinism

Liang Qichao was the most widely read Chinese writer in the first decade of the twentieth century and his ideas shaped the consciousness of a whole generation of Chinese intellectuals. He happened to be the first person to introduce Friedrich Nietzsche to Chinese readers. On October 16, 1902 Liang Qichao, an exile in Japan at the time, published an essay in the *Journal of People's Renovation*, a influential Chinese magazine of which he was the founder, editor and main contributor. In the essay, he quoted Benjamin Kidd, a British sociologist, as saying:

> Evolution points to the future. The past and the present should be treated as no more than vehicles for the transition. Unfortunately contemporary political scientists and sociologists, despite their differences, all pay too much attention on the present while neglecting the future.... The most influential schools of thought in Germany today are Marx's socialism and Nietzsche's individualism. For Marx the main issue of current society is the oppression of the majority of the weak by the minority of the strong. For Nietzsche the problem lies in the restrictions imposed by the majority of the inferior on the minority of the superior. Although both theories are well argued and reasonable, they are geared to the present, and have nothing to do with the future.

About Nietzsche Liang Qichao inserted a note in the essay:

> Nietzsche was an extremist advocate of the right of the strong. He died insane two years ago. His thought has a major impact on Europe and is viewed as a new religion arising at the end of the 19th century.[1]

As its title—"Kidd: A Revolutionary of the Theory of Evolution" suggests, the essay's main subject is neither Nietzsche nor Marx, but

Benjamin Kidd. Liang Qichao presented Kidd as the latest and greatest representative of the theory of evolution. He credited him for having supplied answers to the "two most important questions in the world" which all other thinkers, including Marx and Nietzsche, failed to answer: How mankind would be able to achieve evolution in the future and where evolution would lead mankind. According to the essay, Kidd's answer to the first question was that, in order to succeed in evolution, members of a species must be willing to sacrifice both their individual interest and the collective interest of the current generation for the long term interest of the species, that is, for the interest of "numerous unborn future generations."[2] Liang Qichao did not discuss Kidd's answer to the second of the "two most important questions in the world," which should have been covered in a sequence that he had promised but never completed.*

What Liang Qichao presented was indeed a simplistic picture of Western thought: Marx stands for the collective interest of the majority of the current generation, Nietzsche for individuals and for an elite minority of the current generation, Benjamin Kidd for "future generations" of mankind. Liang Qichao did neither explain why a species' current and future generations must have conflicting interests nor elaborate on why both Marx and Nietzsche were considered "well argued and reasonable," if they were mistaken after all. It is also obvious that whenever he talked about Western concepts such as socialism or individualism, it was merely in vaguest terms. The essay in question seems to be full of superficialities.

The British writer Benjamin Kidd, while not a profound thinker, was far more sophisticated than how he was portrayed by the Chinese author. At the turn of the century, he was a well-known sociologist and writer whose books had been translated into several other languages. In the *Social Evolution* (1894), the first of his two major works, he made frequent references to Karl Marx when criticizing modern liberal thinking. On the one hand, he cited Marx to support his view that the liberal ideal of "the greatest happiness of the greatest number" was no more than an illusion under capitalism and he predicted that Western societies would eventually collapse if unabated competition was allowed to continue. On the other hand, he perceived Marxian socialism as a logical consequence of liberalism, that threatened the established social order in the West and the world dominance of the West. Benjamin Kidd called for a return to religion,

---

* The reason he did not write the sequence is explained on page 11.

especially Christianity in its Protestant form, which, in his view, puts the interest of society and race above that of individuals. He believed that a reconciliation of different social classes within Western societies will strengthen the West, thereby assuring its unfettered "utilization" of the world's natural resources.[3]

The comments on Nietzsche and Marx attributed to Kidd in the Chinese essay are based on the *Principles of Western Civilisation* (1902), Kidd's second major work. In this book, Kidd warned his readers of what he saw as dangerous trends in economy and politics. As if echoing Karl Marx, he argued that unregulated competition would lead to monopoly which in turn would eliminate the very condition of free competition. He also invoked Nietzsche to support his own misgivings about universal suffrage, liberalism, democracy and the socialist movement. Despite his indebtedness to Marx and Nietzsche, he considered both as representing the same "materialistic" preoccupation with prevailing power relations:

> To Nietzsche, as is well known, the modern world is merely a world in which the real masters and superiors have been robbed of their rights—a world in which the *Übermenschen*, the natural ruling caste, have been drugged and anæsthetised by the sentiments and beliefs of our Civilisation into yielding their position to a democracy of whom they are the natural superiors, and against whom they would otherwise be immeasurably the stronger.... But to Marx equally, in the last analysis, it is might only which is right.... For there is in Marx's theories... only the blind growth of the productive forces and the resulting necessity, as Marx conceives it, for the dominance in the end of the interests with which he is concerned. In the one case, as in the other, the standpoint is, therefore, the same: we ultimately stand face to face in the historical process with but one characteristic principle—the ascendancy of the present, and the elimination from society of every cause, sentiment, principle and belief which prevents the strongest interest in the present from realizing itself.[4]

Kidd believed that it was necessary to create conditions that guarantee "a free conflict of interests" among both nations and individuals. To prevent monopoly within a nation, he conceived of a "collective organisation—under the direction of a highly centralised and informed intelligence... of all the activities of industry and production, moving steadily towards the goal of the endowment of all human capacities in a free conflict of forces." Regarding international relations he advocated free trade and an open market and envisioned a "universal empire" built upon these principles, with the "English-speaking peoples" playing a leading role.[5]

It is obvious that, as an introduction to Kidd's thought, Liang Qichao's 1902 essay was a miserable failure. However the essay cannot be dismissed as merely a piece of evidence pointing to the primitive status of the early Chinese reception of Western ideas. When one carefully examines Liang Qichao's intellectual background and the historical context in which he wrote the essay, one realizes that Liang Qichao's seemingly banal references to Marx, Nietzsche and Kidd actually carry quite weighty thoughts.

Liang Qichao was born in 1873 to a farmer's family in Canton. He began to study Confucian classics and history from his parents and grandfather at an early age. A prodigy and with good luck, he had passed both the county level and the provincial level civil service examinations by the age of sixteen. At such a young age, he was already in a position to prepare for the highest scholarly degree that would qualify him for a top position in China's administrative system.

However, he was destined to play a role far greater than that of a successful bureaucrat serving the Qing court. In 1890 he met Kang Youwei, a charismatic and eccentric scholar and social thinker, and was immediately won over by his unconventional views about Confucianism and China's current situation.* He soon enrolled in Kang Youwei's private school, where, over the next four years, he followed a well-rounded and stimulating curriculum Kang Youwei had designed for his students. Liang Qichao's outlook was first of all shaped by the ideas of Kang Youwei, his first major intellectual influence.

Kang Youwei built his theory on a radical reinterpretation of the Confucian tradition. Drawing on earlier exegetic works, he declared some key Confucian texts to be either forged or incomplete. In his view, Confucius, recognizing that his noble ideas did not stand a chance to be understood or accepted in his own time, had embedded them in certain historical and philosophical books for the future generations. Confucius' hidden messages had remained in obscurity for more than two millennia until they were brought to light by Kang Youwei.

Based on a passage from the *Book of Rites*, a classic erroneously attributed to Confucius, Kang Youwei maintained that Confucius saw the

---

* Kang Youwei (1857-1927) was also a Canton native. He is remembered mainly as a reformer who masterminded the Hundred Days Reform in 1898 and as a utopian socialist.

history of mankind as a three-stage process: the "Age of Disorder," the "Age of Ascending Peace" and the "Age of Great Peace." (The last two stages are also respectively called the "Age of Moderate Prosperity" and the "Age of Great Oneness.") The first two stages are characterized by men exploiting and oppressing other men, nations waging wars against other nations. In these two stages mankind and other creatures all live in misery and the world is like a "slaughterhouse." To deliver the world from suffering, many "sages" and thinkers have been looking for remedies. Although some of them have found ways to ameliorate particular problems, none of them has offered a fundamental solution. Their outlook is confined to the first two historical stages and they fail to recognize that no real changes can occur under current moralities and laws that have been created by the strong to maintain their domination.[6] Only Confucius has looked beyond the first two historical stages and prepared entirely new laws and ethical principles for mankind. The teaching of Confucius will deliver mankind from suffering once and for all and bring in the "Age of Great Oneness." Kang Youwei's society of "Great Oneness" is a socialist utopia where national and racial boundaries no longer exist, all men and women live in equality and enjoy comfort and freedom with the help of technology.[7]

Although credited to Confucius, Kang Youwei's ideas have other origins. His preoccupation with the issue of suffering and his thesis that man suffers because he fails to recognize the oneness of all lives are directly borrowed from Buddhism. His socialist utopia was also inspired by his knowledge of the West. When he visited Hong Kong in 1879, he was impressed by the crown colony's buildings, its well maintained streets, and its public order. After contacting Western missionaries and reading their publications, he came to the conclusion that, in addition to other reforms, China needed a religion. Reinventing the Confucian tradition was part of his effort to create a religion for China. The "Age of Great Oneness" was Kang Youwei's counterpart of the Christian millennium. Kang Youwei's socialist utopia can be seen as a happy union of ancient traditions of the East on the one hand and Christian values, liberal-democratic ideals and modern technology of the West on the other hand. Liang Qichao was among the few students who learned about these ideas and he embraced them with the zeal of a disciple.

The second major intellectual influence on Liang Qichao came from Yan Fu whom Liang Qichao had referred to as his "most understanding friend" and "the best teacher in the world," aside from his father and Kang

Youwei."[8] Yan Fu was one of the first Chinese students who were sent abroad by the Qing government to study technology. During his stay in England between 1876 and 1879 as a student of naval science, he had developed a keen interest in Western thought, an interest he continued to pursue after returning to China. In the aftermath of the Sino-Japanese War (1894–1895), Yan Fu had become a unique political writer who freely drew on Charles Darwin, Adam Smith, Herbert Spencer and other Western thinkers to support the cause of reform. His greatest contribution, however, was the book *On the Evolution of Heaven*, a milestone in the intellectual history of modern China.

On the Evolution of Heaven is partly based on Thomas Henry Huxley's *Evolution and Ethics*. Yan Fu must have found Huxley's book a convenient starting point, for it contains a succinct and poetic presentation of Charles Darwin's theory as well as a historical survey of the idea of evolution that covers ancient Greek philosophers, Buddhism and modern European thinkers. Yan Fu, however, did not agree with the main point Huxley made in *Evolution and Ethics*. Huxley criticized social Darwinists such as Herbert Spencer for treating social relations as a purely natural phenomenon. Human relationships, he argued, should not be governed by power relations but by ethical values. In *On the Evolution of Heaven*, Yan Fu argued that nature and human society are part of the same cosmic process that evolves progressively through the mechanism of natural selection. Therefore there is nothing incompatible between evolution and ethics.

Strictly speaking, Yan Fu was not a social Darwinist, as many Chinese and Western scholars have believed. Although he spoke in a quasi-Darwinist language, the theory he had formulated bears more imprints of Chinese ideas and values than anything else. Either in the Taoist tradition or the Confucian tradition, nature and human society have never been viewed as two separate and impermeable realms. Nature affects human society, and vice versa. Yan Fu did not express a foreign idea when he asserted that the natural order and the ethical order go hand in hand. It is not accidental that Yan Fu translated the phrase "natural selection" into "Heaven's selection," for the latter is just a variation of the ancient Chinese notion of the "Mandate of Heaven." Yan Fu can be viewed as a social Darwinist only in the sense that he was willing to apply the theory of evolution to human society. Otherwise the theory he formulated in *On the Evolution of Heaven* is the opposite of social Darwinism in spirit and should be better characterized as a reverse social Darwinism. Yan Fu attributed European prosperity to international competition among European nations, which he characterized as a process that "begins with jealousy but ends with benefiting all."⁹ In such a process, no nation is inherently "unfit." If only a nation makes changes and adapts itself to the ever changing conditions, it will be fit for survival in the process of "Heaven's selection." He translated the Spencerian phrase "survival of the fittest" into "survival of the fit," implying the possibility of coexistence. Thus social Darwinism, a theory that rationalizes the domination of the strong was reversed into one that encourages the weak to get strong.

With the memory of the Sino-Japanese War fresh, Chinese intellectuals found in Yan Fu's book both a warning and a message of hope. Liang Qichao read the manuscript of Yan Fu's *On the Evolution of Heaven* in 1896. Already a well-known spokesman for the reform movement, he began to invoke the immutable law of the "evolution of Heaven" as a rationale for reform, cautioning that the Chinese would risk "extinction" as a species if they did not make necessary changes fast enough.

For the time being, however, Yan Fu's influence on Liang Qichao was overshadowed by that of Kang Youwei. Liang Qichao embraced Yan Fu's ideas inasmuch as they were compatible with what he had learned from Kang Youwei. Otherwise he stood by his mentor Kang Youwei. One example was his attitude toward Yan Fu's idea of "public morality [公德]." Yan Fu believed that the power and wealth of the West was built upon "public morality"— people's willingness to identify their individual private interests with the national public interests. Obviously "public morality" was Yan Fu's rendition of the English word "nationalism." Yan Fu wrongly believed that the West had developed nationalism through "sociology," a word he translated into Chinese as the "study of group formation [群學]."

Liang Qichao rejected the idea of "public morality," which, he thought, was too narrowly defined. In his view, one should neither completely overlook individuals' private interests nor should one be concerned exclusively with the interests of one's own nation. On the other hand, he was fascinated by the phrase "group formation," which he declared it to be a universal principle. He viewed the history of mankind as the application of this principle on an ever broader scale. He criticized the West for applying the principle of "group formation" only to nations, instead of to mankind. In his view a "world group" would eventually be formed in the "Age of Great Oneness."¹⁰

Liang Qichao fled to Japan in 1898 after the Hundred Days Reform failed. He quickly learned to read Japanese and began to explore Western philosophical, political and social ideas through Japanese sources. Liang Qichao described himself as being turned into a "new person that speaks a new language and thinks in new terms" through reading Japanese books.[11] The "new person," however, was not entirely new. Japanese books had moved him away from Kang Youwei to a position very close to Yan Fu. He began to speak and think like Yan Fu. Now he also viewed "natural selection" and "the superior triumphing over the inferior" as principles governing social relations.[12] He agreed with Yan Fu that China's priority was to nurture nationalism by cultivating "public morality" among its people. Yan Fu had borrowed the phrase "people's renovation" from the *Great Learning*, a Confucian classic, to characterize his project of importing nationalism from the West. When Liang Qichao founded a journal in 1902 to advocate reform, he called it the "*Journal of People's Renovation.*"

Liang Qichao had not completely given up what he had learned from Kang Youwei. Through reading Japanese sources, he was able to wed Kang Youwei's utopian socialism with Yan Fu's reverse social Darwinism. Liang Qichao had learned from Kato Hiroyuki that "there is no such thing as right in the world... only power counts" and that it is "a universal principle of evolution" that the strong wields power over the weak.*[13] On the other hand, he fully agreed with Rudolf von Jhering that people must resist aggression in order to protect their rights and that "rights are maintained by continual efforts"†[14] Based on these two premises and other ideas he had acquired from Japanese sources, Liang Qichao recast Kang Youwei's three historical stages into a new theory of history. According to this theory, the "Age of Disorder" is a time when society is not divided into the strong and the weak or the rulers and the ruled yet. Gradually due to social differentiation, certain groups of men begin to wield power over other groups and certain

---

* Kato Hiroyuki [1836-1916] a Japanese political theorist, best known for his early introduction of Rousseau's democratic ideas, his later turn to conservatism and his advocacy of social Darwinism.

† Rudolf von Jhering [1818-1892] German legal scholar, among his main works are *The Spirit of the Roman Law* and *Law As a Means to an End*. Liang Qichao translated the German word "Recht," which can mean either "right" or "law," into a Chinese word [權利] that means only "right." Liang Qichao did not give the Japanese source from which he had learned about Rudolf von Jhering.

individuals over other individuals, thus giving rise to "the Age of Ascending Peace." Eventually the weak social groups stand up against those who have previously monopolized power. For example, the labor has acquired equal status with the capital through an "economic revolution," and women have achieved equality with men through a "feminist revolution." These revolutions will usher in the "Age of Great Oneness," culminating in equality among all peoples in the world.[15] It seems that while Yan Fu had reversed social Darwinism and made it a "to live and let live" philosophy, Liang Qichao had given the reverse social Darwinism a radical tone, turning it into a theory of revolution.

Having examined Liang Qichao's intellectual background, we are in a better position to assess his 1902 essay on Benjamin Kidd. First of all, we recognize in Liang Qichao a good pupil of Kang Youwei in his attitude toward books. Just as his mentor had used ancient Chinese classics to create a socialist utopia, a new religion, Liang Qichao used Western thinkers mainly to advance his own social and political agenda. If we examine a dozen or so essays on Western thinkers written by him in 1902 and 1903, we realize that whether he talked about Jeremy Bentham, Immanuel Kant, Benjamin Kidd, or any other Western thinker, he was merely using them to illustrate and justify his own theory of "people's renovation." We probably should not assume that he intentionally falsified what he had read. It may be that his lack of proficiency in Japanese combined with his political zeal made him unable to distinguish what he had read into the texts from what the texts actually contain.

Liang Qichao was drawn to Benjamin Kidd partially due to a misidentification. Three years before he wrote his essay on Kidd, the *Global News*, a missionary publication in China, had introduced Kidd's book *Social Evolution* (1894) to Chinese readers in a synopsis. The authors of the synopsis used the phrase "Great Oneness" to characterize Kidd's social ideal.[16] This must have led Liang Qichao to view Benjamin Kidd as the Western counterpart of Kang Youwei, a champion of a socialist utopia. Moreover, Benjamin Kidd in his *Principles of Western Civilisation* presented himself as the only thinker who was concerned with the future instead of the present, a role that Confucius had played according to Kang Youwei. Besides, Kidd was speaking a language familiar to Liang Qichao— the language of social Darwinism. All these led Liang Qichao to treat Kidd as the most important thinker in the world.

As a Confucian scholar influenced by Kang Youwei's utopian socialism, Liang Qichao naturally considered Marx's concern for social justice to be "well argued and reasonable." Also because of his Confucian background and his apprenticeship with Kang Youwei, Liang Qichao perceived himself as part of an elite on a mission to liberate the Chinese and mankind. He could not agree more with Nietzsche in decrying the "restrictions imposed by the majority of the inferior on the minority of the superior." For him the failed Hundred Days Reform of 1898 must appear to be such a case. He was so frustrated with the "majority of inferior" that he regarded the "four hundred million heartless, brainless, and spineless people" as the worst obstacle to progress. His *Journal of People's Renovation* was created for the very purpose to enlighten this inferior majority, a near hopeless task which he took upon himself nevertheless.[17]

Liang Qichao did not understand Kidd's argument but had his own reason to consider both Marx and Nietzsche to be "geared to the present" and "have nothing to do with the future." From Japanese sources Liang Qichao had learned that European nations had adopted "national imperialism" toward weak nations and a few big capitalists would soon monopolize the world's production and natural resources, thereby enslaving the rest of mankind.[18] With such an imminent danger in mind, Liang Qichao must have seen Marx and Nietzsche as too much concerned with present issues such as social justice and the ascendance of the superior in a society. In his view the "most urgent task" was to "nurture nationalism" by "renovating" the Chinese people.[19] Nationalism of oppressed nations, he believed, was the only effective means to defeat "national imperialism." Mankind would have a future only when all nations had become equally strong and treat each other as equal partners. That would be the "Age of Great Oneness."

Liang Qichao seemed to be more critical of Nietzsche than of Marx. The only problem with Marx was the issue of priority. Nietzsche's view, in addition to its wrong priority, was problematic for two other reasons. He was described in Liang Qichao's essay as representing individualism and as "an extremist advocate of the right of the strong." Liang Qichao, influenced by Kang Youwei, had once believed in "individualism." But when he wrote the essay, he had already abandoned "individualism" and was mainly concerned with how "to train the people and lead them to victory in the arena of competition."[20] Liang Qichao, being a reverse social Darwinist, believed in the right of the strong but also in the weak gaining rights through self-strengthening. He certainly disapproved "an extremist advocate of the right of the strong," that is, a typical social Darwinist.

Liang Qichao's 1902 essay covers only the first few pages of *Social Evolution* and the first three of the eleven chapters of the *Principles of Western Civilization*. It was apparently written before its author had finished reading the latter book. Liang Qichao must have soon realized that Kidd did not share his ideal of "Great Oneness" but supported the domination of the West. In the next issue of the *Journal of People's Renovation*, instead of continuing his essay on Kidd, as he had promised, he wrote a futuristic short story about a "new China," a republic founded in 1912, hosting a peace conference of the United Nations in 1962. Among the leaders coming from all over the world to sign a peace treaty were a Russian president, a Philippine president and a Hungarian president.[21] This dream of a family of independent and democratic nations, with China playing a central role in promoting peace, can be seen as Liang Qichao's answer to the question "Whither evolution will lead mankind," one that was very different from Kidd's answer. Liang Qichao was unwilling to take back what he had said about Kidd. He simply stopped talking about Kidd from then on, leaving many of his readers, including Mao Zedong, with the notion that Kidd was the greatest thinker in the world.*

Liang Qichao had no interest in Nietzsche per se. His knowledge of the German philosopher did not go beyond Kidd's book and, perhaps, some encyclopedias or textbooks. He would have never mentioned Nietzsche in the *Journal of People's Renovation*, if he had not mistaken Kidd for a kindred spirit. He needed Nietzsche and Marx to bear out Kidd's importance, just as he needed Kidd to promote his own reverse social Darwinism and revolutionary nationalism.

Liang Qichao's views about social Darwinism and about history in general underwent dramatic changes as the result of his trip to Europe in 1919. Having witnessed a Europe devastated by the war and afflicted with social strife, he arrived at the conclusion that international competition and competition within a society do not necessarily lead to progress, as he and Yan Fu had believed. He stopped trying to "renovate" the Chinese by teaching them nationalism. Instead, he thought the Chinese should "cultivate their inherited spirit of cooperation" rather than "accept the principle of national rivalry." He warned the Chinese against narrow-

---

* See p. 82

minded patriotism and recommended that they build a "cosmopolitan country," with the goal of "fully developing the natural endowments of all individuals within the framework of the state, while contributing to the common culture of mankind."[22]

To express these new ideas more effectively and forcefully, Liang Qichao found Nietzsche convenient again, although he had made no reference to the German philosopher for nearly twenty years since his 1902 essay. He called Nietzsche's philosophy "a malignant form of egoism" that could be traced to Max Stirner and Sören Kierkegaard. He asserted that "Nietzsche regarded altruism as a slave morality and the strong preying upon the weak a precondition for progress"; that Nietzsche's philosophy implied "worship of power and money" and it had turned militarism and imperialism into "the most fashionable policy"; and that Nietzsche's philosophy must be held responsible for the Great War and for the "future class war in each country."[23] These comments did not arise from a better understanding of Nietzsche. Liang Qichao was merely repeating what other Chinese had said about Nietzsche in newspapers and journals.*

Since then Liang Qichao devoted himself to the study of China's intellectual heritage. Over the next few years before his death in 1929 he wrote some of the best works in his life. His later writings, however, were largely ignored by the public. The mood of the nation had changed: the younger generation that had been "renovated" by his reverse social Darwinism began to make revolution. Even today Liang Qichao is still remembered by most people for his early writings in the *People's Renovation*. As prophet of the twentieth century revolution in China, Liang Qichao's contribution to modern Chinese history can hardly be overestimated. As interpreter of Western thought, however, he set a bad precedent for later generations. He made it fashionable for intellectuals to talk unabashedly about Western thinkers without first studying their ideas and he introduced the habit of using Western thinkers as stereotypes to convey one's own ideas. Even in today's China, Liang Qichao is still something to be overcome for many intellectuals.

---

* He may have read essays about Nietzsche by Chen Duxiu, Lin Shuang and Cai Yuanpei. See p. 31 and p. 82.

Notes

[1] Liang Qichao, "Kidd: A Revolutionary of the Theory of Evolution," in Liang Qichao, *Collected Works of Liang Qichao* [《飲冰室文集》], ed. Lin Zhijun (Taipei: Zhonghuo Shuju, 1960), vol. 5, issue 12, 84-86

[2] *Ibid.*, 78-79.

[3] Benjamin Kidd, *Social Evolution* (Chicago: Charles H. Sergel Company, 1894), 107-108, 259-269, 288-289.

[4] Benjamin Kidd, *Principles of Western Civilisation* (London: MacMillan and Co. Limited, 1902), 91-94, 96-97, 128-131.

[5] *Ibid.*, 478-481.

[6] Wang Xiaobo, et al., *Kang Youwei and Liang Qichao*, Modern Chinese Thinkers Series, No. 3 [王曉波，李日章，李容中等編，《現代中國思想家》第三集《康有為，梁起超》] (Taipei: Giant Press, 1978), 137–139.

[7] Also see Liang Qichao, *Liang Qichao's Works by Categories* [《飲冰室類編》] (Taipei: Huazheng Books, 1974), vol. 2, 384-416.

[8] Liang Qichao, "Letter to Yan Fu," *Collected Works*, vol. 1, 107.

[9] Yan Fu, *Selected Essays and Poems of Yan Fu* [周振甫選注，《嚴復詩文選》] (Beijing, People's Literature Press, 1959), 22.

[10] Liang Qichao, *Collected Works*, vol. 1, 106-111 and vol. 2, 3-6.

[11] Ding Wenjiang and Zhao Fengtian, *The Life of Liang Qichao: Selected Sources in Chronological Order* (Shanghai: People Press, 1983) [丁文江，趙丰田，《梁任公先生年譜長篇》], 189.

[12] Liang Qichao, *Collected Works*, vol. 5, issue 13, 9.

[13] *Ibid.*, vol. 4, issue 10, 29; and *Liang Qichao's Works by Categories*, vol. 2, 178-179.

[14] Liang Qichao, *Liang Qichao's Works by Categories* [《飲冰室類編》] (Taipei: Huazheng Books, 1974), vol. 1, 133.

[15] Liang Qichao, *Collected Works*, vol. 4, issue 10, 29–33.

[16] Beijing University, Dept. of Philosophy, *Selected Sources of Contemporary Chinese Philosophy*, (Beijing: Beijing University Press, 1988), 3-5. The synopsis was written by Richard Timothy, a British missionary, and Cai Erkang, a Chinese scholar.

[17] Liang Qichao, *Works by Categories*, Vol. 2, 869.

[18] *Ibid.*, vol 1, 418-428 ("A Comparative Study of the Idea of State"); and *Ibid.*, vol 1, 543 and 541.

[19] *Ibid.*, vol. 1, 105.

[20] *Ibid.*, vol 2, 394.

[21] *Ibid.*, vol. 2. 856–867.

[22] Liang Qichao, *Recent Works of Liang Qichao (vol. 1)* [《梁任公近著》] (Taipei: Wenhai Press, 1978), 38-39.

[23] *Ibid.*, 16-17.

CHAPTER 2

Wang Guowei:

A Nietzsche That Is Believable But Not Lovable

Liang Qichao was looked up by most of his contemporaries as an expert on Western thought. One person, however, challenged his authority. In 1905 a writer named Wang Guowei wrote for the journal *The World of Education*:

> Since 1900 there have appeared quite a number of journals, whose contributors are either rebel students or fugitives in exile. These are politically motivated publications that have little to do with scholarship. Whenever they discuss scholarly matters, they merely plagiarize or give fragmented information. An essay on Kant in the *Journal of People's Renovation* is such an example. Eighty to ninety percent of its content is misrepresentation. . . If these people are interested in politics, why don't they simply discuss politics, instead of desecrating philosophy?[1]

The essay in question, "The Teachings of Kant—the Greatest Philosopher in Modern Times," was written by Liang Qichao. It portrays Immanuel Kant as a prophet of nationalism who had "renovated" the German people with a new morality and thereby enabled Germany to become a powerful nation.[2] It is fair to characterize such an essay as "eighty to ninety percent" "misrepresentation."

Wang Guowei regarded philosophical inquiries as a sacred profession. He was indignant at those who hindered the seeking of philosophical truth, be they political dissidents or government authorities. When he learned that a senior official in charge of educational reform had excluded philosophy from university curriculum, he made a sarcastic remark:

> We must applaud the governor-general [referring to Zhang Zhidong (1837-1909), governor-general of Hunan and Hubei] who appears much wiser than

European politicians. Schopenhauer once said, "Academic philosophy is the death of truth." Indeed true philosophy does not exist in universities. It prospers only through independent studies. How fortunate it is for philosophy to be eliminated by the governor-general!³

Wang Guowei believed that all scholarly pursuits have their intrinsic values and must not be treated as a means to other ends. It dismayed him to see that Western philosophy was rejected by the conservative bureaucrats and distorted by political dissidents. He respected Yen Fu for his knowledge in Western thought. But Yen Fu was mainly interested in economics and sociology, not in philosophy. Wang Guowei was pessimistic about the future of Western philosophy in China:

> I am certain that there is no one [in China] who understands the profound and noble ideas of the Europeans. Even if there is such a person, I am certain that he cannot make himself known. Besides, in recent years, those who have studied abroad are either full of political ambition or only concerned with practical subjects. It is obvious that even if there were someone willing to exert himself over impractical and exhausting philosophical issues, he would have been unable to make the least impact on the scholarly world.⁴

At the time he made these comments, he had already been studying Western philosophy for some time. It seemed that he was willing to sacrifice himself for philosophical truth. Wang Guowei was one of the rare Chinese writers in the early 20th century who made earnest efforts to understand basic Western philosophical categories. He was the first Chinese to read and analyze Nietzsche and to quote him in his own writings.

Born in Haining, Jiangsu province in 1876, Wang Guowei's education in his childhood was similar to that of Liang Qichao, though he was less lucky with the civil service examinations. As many Chinese intellectuals, he was influenced by Kang Youwei's ideas on reform after the Sino-Japanese War. Wang Guowei left home for Shanghai in early 1898 and worked for a few months as a clerk for *Current Affairs*, a reform journal founded by Liang Qichao. Later in the same year he enrolled in the Eastern Languages School where he came under a very different influence.

The two cofounders of the Eastern Languages School, Luo Zhenyu and Jiang Fu, were also part of the late Qing reform movement.* In the aftermath of the Sino-Japanese War, they founded the Society of

---

* Lo Zhengyu (1866-1940) was a philologist, archaeologist, and scholar of Chinese classics; Jiang Fu (1866-1911) was a Confucian scholar.

Agriculture to introduce agricultural technologies from Wesern countries and Japan. Later, in 1898, they created the Eastern Languages School to train translators for the society. Luo Zhenyu and Jiang Fu recognized that China would not be able to survive as a sovereign state without reforms. But compared with Kang Youwei and Liang Qichao, they were more conservative in moral and political outlooks. For one thing, they were too erudite in Chinese classical texts and too committed to Confucian values to be taken in by Kang Youwei's radical reinterpretation of the Confucian tradition. Rather than initiating fundamental changes in the name of reform, they promoted reform in order to preserve China's polity, ideas, and values.

The Eastern languages School hired two Japanese scholars as its instructors, a move that reflected its founders' outlook. Fujita Toyohachi (1869–1929), the chief instructor, was an authority on classical Chinese literature, highly respected in both Japan and China. Taoka Sayoji (1870–1912, also known as Taoka Reiun), the English instructor, was a critic of nationalism, social Darwinism and the materialistic tendency of the nineteenth century Europe. He relished an aesthetic socialist vision inspired by China's remote past.[5]

Both Japanese scholars were well versed in Western philosophy. Wang Guowei was filled with admiration when, one day in 1899, he read excerpts of Kant and Schopenhauer in Taoka Sayoji's writings. At the time he was unsure whether he would ever be able to read the two German philosophers himself, for he had learned Japanese for only one year and had known even less English. The seed of the love for philosophy, however, was sown in his heart.[6]

The Eastern Languages School was closed in 1900 due to the Boxer Uprising. Wang Guowei was sent to Japan to continue his study by Luo Zhenyu, now his patron. Soon after his arrival in Japan, Wang Guowei fell sick and had to return to China in the summer of 1901. It was then that he began to study Western philosophy, guided by Fujita Toyohachi, his former instructor in the Eastern Languages School. Many years later Toyohachi remembered Wang Guowei as a promising pupil "whose Japanese was excellent and whose English was good as well and who had, moreover, a profound interest in the study of Western philosophy."[7]

In 1903, after spending more than a year reading introductory books, both in Japanese and in English, he began to read Kant's *Critique of Pure Reason*. The book proved to be too difficult for him. He could proceed no further than the section on "Transcendental Analytic," which completely baffled him. He then turned to Schopenhauer and was fascinated by him. From the summer of 1903 to the winter of 1904, he always had Schopenhauer's books by his side. In addition to *The World as Will and Idea* which he read twice, he also read *On the Fourfold Root of the Principle of Sufficient Reason, On the Will in Nature*, and other works by the German philosopher.

Wang Guowei admired Schopenhauer for his eloquent style and incisive observations, but he rejected Schopenhauer's idea of the "annulment of the Will." In his essay "Comments on *Dreams in the Red Mansion*," (summer 1904) Wang Guowei reasoned that if the "Will to Live" of an individual is only part of the "Will to Live" of the whole—Nature as thing-in-itself, as Schopenhauer himself believed, then "unless all men and all other creatures in the universe annul their Will to Live, the Will of an individual cannot possibly be annulled."[8] When Schopenhauer invoked the Bible, Buddhist sutras and some other texts to prove that man has the divine mission to deliver all other creatures from suffering, Wang Guowei made the following comments:

> Mr. Schopenhauer quoted the classics in vain. These classics give no theoretical support to him. We want to ask: since Buddha achieved nirvana, since Jesus Christ died on the cross, what has become of the Will to Live of men and all other things? What has become of their suffering? I believe that they are no different now from what they were before. Are we still to wait for the promised good men to bring all created things to God?* Or is it a self-deceiving theory which can never be realized? If it is the latter, it is far from clear that Buddha or Jesus Christ have delivered themselves from suffering.[9]

We do not know when Wang Guowei began to read Nietzsche and whether his criticism of Schopenhauer was partly influenced by Nietzsche. It seems that in the beginning his interest in Nietzsche was secondary to his admiration for Schopenhauer. Nietzsche had written an essay "Schopenhauer as an Educator," in which he argued that Schopenhauer should serve as an educator for youth because he was able to rise to greatness despite the petty and decadent bourgeois society in which he

---

* Schopenhauer quoted Meister Eckhart as saying "I bear witness to the saying of Christ. I, if I be lifted up from the earth, will draw all things unto me (John xii. 32). So shall the good man draw all things up to God... A good man brings to God one created thing in the other." See Arthur Schopenhauer, *The World As Will and Idea*, London: Routledge & Paul Ltd., 1883 (Ninth impression, 1950), Book 4, 491-492.

lived. Wang Guowei had merely heard of the essay which he assumed to be about Schopenhauer's views on education. He took upon himself to write on the same subject and the result was his essay "Schopenhauer's philosophy and his theory on education." In his essay Wang Guowei deduced a whole set of pedagogical principles from Schopenhauer's philosophy.[10] The essay proves to be an extraordinary feat for a Chinese student of Western philosophy and it contains brilliant ideas about education that may well have been endorsed by Schopenhauer himself.

In time Wang Guowei became more and more attracted to Nietzsche and he felt the need to define his own position in regard to Schopenhauer and Nietzsche. In his 1904 essay "Schopenhauer and Nietzsche," he made two main points: Nietzsche's philosophy is an elaboration of Schopenhauer's philosophy and Schopenhauer is not what he appears to be, but actually a Nietzsche in disguise.[11]

According to Wang Guowei, Nietzsche agrees with Schopenhauer in viewing the Will as the essence of existence, but he rejects the latter's ethics that is based on the annulment of the Will. It appears to Nietzsche that the Will to annul the Will is still a Will. Nietzsche has developed his own ethics on the basis of Schopenhauer's esthetics. Just as a Schopenhauerian genius is unrestrained by sufficient reason in his artistic creations, a Nietzschean superman is not bound by moral principles in his deeds. Wang Guowei found further evidence of kinship between the two German philosophers when he compared the spirit's three metamorphoses from *Thus Spoke Zarathustra* with Schopenhauer's remarks on the child-like character of genius. Schopenhauerian genius is like a child whose intellect has developed ahead of its other organs, especially its genitals, and who therefore is able to look at the world with pure objectivity; similarly a Nietzschean superman-child enjoys complete freedom since he is motivated by a will unbridled by ethics.

If Nietzsche's philosophy is built upon that of Schopenhauer, is it the better of the two? Wang Guowei did not take sides and he tried to prove that there are actually no substantial differences between the two. Wang Guowei made a flawed comparison of the private lives of the two German philosophers. By quoting from Paulsen's *System of Ethics*, he tried to show that Schopenhauer, despite his call for the annulment of the Will and his espousal of universal love, was a stingy and mean-spirited person who indulged in sensual pleasures. Then he quoted from Windelband's *History of Philosophy*:

> What [Nietzsche] sought is happiness, either through knowledge or through power. He was exhausted by the struggle between these two pursuits. When he was older, he could no longer content himself with impersonal and superpersonal values, such as intellectual, aesthetic, or moral values. Instead he tried to gain infinite power in his real life.

This turns out to be a mistranslation. According to the original text, Windelband was not making a comment on Nietzsche's personal life, but his relation to his age,

> The enjoyment which he [Nietzsche] seeks is either that of knowing or that of power. In the struggle between the two he has been crushed—the victim of an age which is satisfied no longer by the impersonal and superpersonal values of intellectual, aesthetic, and moral culture, but thirsts again for the boundless unfolding of the individual in a life of deeds.[12]

After reaching the wrong conclusion that both Schopenhauer and Nietzsche were mainly concerned with materialistic interests, Wang Guowei tried to understand why they had invented their systems of metaphysics. He reasoned that while both philosophers were great geniuses with a strong will and a powerful intellect, they, just as everyone else, were subjected to various conditions that limited their will and intellect. Because they were unable to enjoy small pleasures in life that console average men, they, as geniuses, suffered far more than average men. They ended up in turning to philosophy for imaginary fulfillment:

> They have to see themselves as emperors and as God and to look down on others as ants and feces. They are sons of nature but desire to be its mother; they are slaves of nature but desire to be its master. They try to discard, minimize, dismember, burn, and destroy anything that limits their "will" and "intellect." It is not that they can actually accomplish such things, but that they simply say so and take pleasure in saying so. They are not speaking to others but simply amusing themselves. Why? With the enormity of their intellect and will, and the enormity of their suffering, there would be no other way for them to console themselves.[13]

This psychological explanation was followed by a theoretical analysis. Schopenhauer, wrote Wang Guowei, had brought Kantian epistemology to its logical conclusion. Schopenhauer perceived the phenomenal world as our idea and identified the noumenal world with our will. As we and the universe are representations of the same Will, the universal Will is at the same time our will. Therefore we experience the universe not only through our intellect but also through our will. But such a profoundly experienced universe still could not satiate Schopenhauer who was actually seeking to grasp the universe in an absolute way:

> Although Schopenhauer aimed at the annulment of the Will, he also speculated, in the fourth chapter of his great book, that this annulment could never be final. He advocated universal love; but what he loved was not the world, but his own world. He advocated the annulment of the Will, but it was not a real annulment, he was merely dissatisfied with the present world. Such a position is more extreme than Buddha's saying, "Above in heaven and down on earth, the self is the only master." What Schopenhauer wanted was "Above in heaven and down on earth, the self is the only thing that exists.' In working out his theory, Schopenhauer perceived himself as Atlas who shouldered the earth, as Brahma who gave birth to the universe. Herein lay his metaphysical need; herein lay his lifelong consolation. Therefore, across the ages, there has been no one who affirms the Will more thoroughly than Schopenhauer did. However, he revealed his true intention only occasionally through his aesthetic theory of genius.[14]

In contrast to Schopenhauer, Nietzsche went a step further:

> Believing in a positive philosophy, Nietzsche was not satisfied with metaphysical speculation. He endeavored to realize his will in this world rather than in the nonexistent other world; in the material rather than in the nonexistent spiritual. Therefore, in its early phase, Nietzsche's thought was dominated by Schopenhauer's aesthetics. When he was older, he took innocence as his ethical model. Imitating Schopenhauer's theory of genius, he advocated superman; imitating Schopenhauer's rejection of sufficient reason, he rejected morality. Holding his head high, he walked on with long strides, allowing his will to wander playfully in the universe.[15]

Thus both Schopenhauer and Nietzsche were seeking ultimate self-affirmation and self-expansion. The only difference is that Nietzsche was more aware of his real motive and was bold enough to give it full expression. In Wang Guowei's words:

> If we compare Schopenhauer and Nietzsche to a tree: Schopenhauer's theory is the roots reaching deep and spreading wide in the ground; Nietzsche's theory is the branches and leaves, rising high into the heavens, piercing through the clouds. Nietzsche's theory is the three peaks of Taihua [Huashan, a Chinese mountain in the province of Shaanxi], Schopenhauer's theory is the granites beneath the mountain.[16]

Wang Guowei was not necessarily in favor of either Nietzsche or Schopenhauer, although the metaphors just quoted seem to put Nietzsche in a loftier position. Since he viewed philosophic systems as means to deliver people from suffering, a more relevant question for him should be: Which of the two German philosophers had offered a better consolation to the suffering mankind? Wang Guowei did not spell out his answer. He hinted at it by referring to a fable from an ancient Chinese classic:

> The nobleman Yin conducted his business on a large scale. His slaves worked for him from morning to night without rest. There was an old man who was quite feeble but was forced to do even more chores. He worked and moaned in the daytime. In the night when he fell asleep, he would dream that he was a prince ruling a state who leisurely wandered in the palace and enjoyed every imaginable luxury. When waking up, he continued with his drudgery.[17]

The moral, Wang Guowei explained, is that a Schopenhauerian genius suffers just like the old slave awake in the daytime and Schopenhauer's aesthetic elitism and his theory of the universal Will are nothing but the old slave's dreams in the night. Compared with Schopenhauer, Nietzsche had a better grasp of reality:

> Nietzsche was different. With his genius comparable to that of Schopenhauer but without the latter's faith in metaphysics, he remained a slave, day and night, in his dreams and when awake.... Therefore he had to throw off all the burdens and reverse all values. He was going to actualize in the daylight all those things Schopenhauer had used to console himself in dreams. This is why Schopenhauer's theory is, after all, compatible with common moralities while Nietzsche was a most insubordinate rebel.[18]

Two issues are involved here. One is whether the old slave could actually throw off all the burdens imposed on him and become a prince in real life. Wang Guowei's answer seemed to be negative, for he always viewed suffering as part of man's existence and philosophy as man's solace. The second issue, whether the old slave should ever try to throw off burdens, may be more important. The point is not whether he could actually liberate himself but whether his rebellion amounts to a consolation better than dreams. Although Wang Guowei did not give an explicit answer to this question, he indicated his abhorrence of the moral consequence of the Nietzschean solution.

Beside the few essays mainly dealing with philosophy, Wang Guowei's literary criticism and other writings between 1904 and 1907 also reflect the influence of German philosophy. For example he was fond of using such Schopenhauerian-Kantian concepts as "universal forms," "disinterested contemplation," and so on in his review of China's poetical tradition. His contention that philosophy and art in China has been contaminated by ethical and political considerations and his description of an artistic "world without self" [無我之境] seems to be informed by the concept of the Dionysian.[19]

Wang Guowei's 1907 essay "A Study of Hobbies," (1907) can be seen as another attempt to bridge and compare Schopenhauer and Nietzsche, though it mentions neither's name. The essay distinguishes between two kinds of suffering. There is "active suffering" arising from the "Will to Live" as man toils with his hands or his mind to make a living. Once man succeeds in making a living, he will either be subjected to "passive suffering" if he is tormented by ennui due to lack of activity, or he will experience a different kind of "active suffering" if his "Will to Live" is transformed into the "Will to Power," that is, if he tries to excel himself "materially and spiritually" in various "hobbies," such as chess playing, drama, art and literature.[20] Although the essay's central concern is suffering, its anti-asceticism and its activism bring it closer to Nietzsche than to Schopenhauer. It affirms that activities are necessary in order to overcome suffering, for "passive suffering is much more unbearable than "active suffering." In contrast to "passive suffering" that has nothing to offer but ennui, "active suffering" at least promises pleasure in activities in the form of hobbies. In Wang Guowei's words, "It is better to [live and] dislike life than not to live; it is better to dislike activities than not to engage in activities."[21] Here Wang Guowei nearly reached the height of a Dionysian hero.

After reading Schopenhauer and Nietzsche, Wang Guowei was able to understand Kant better and he read *Critique of Pure Reason* three more times by 1905. Just as he seemed to be able to adventure further in the field of Western philosophy, he turned away from it. Here is his explanation:

> I have been tired of philosophy for quite a long time. It is a general rule of all philosophic theories that those that can be loved cannot be believed, and those that can be believed cannot be loved. I want to know the truth, yet I love the absurd. What I love most are great metaphysics, sublime ethics, and pure aesthetics. But in my search for what is believable, I am inclined to believe in the positive theory of truth, the hedonistic theory of ethics, and the empiricist theory of aesthetics. I know these are believable, but I cannot love them. Other theories are lovable, but I cannot believe in them. I have been much vexed by this dilemma in the past two or three years. Recently I have gradually shifted my interest from philosophy to literature where I wish I could find direct consolation.[22]

An examination of Wang's writings between 1904 and 1907 shows that what he called "great metaphysics, sublime ethics, and pure aesthetics" refer to Kant and Schopenhauer, and what he called the "positive theory of truth, the hedonistic theory of ethics, and the empiricist theory of aesthetics" mainly refer to Nietzsche's philosophy.²³ Thus Kant and Schopenhauer are lovable but not believable, Nietzsche is believable but not lovable. Wang Guowei had to choose between the Scylla of beautiful lies and the Charybdis of ugly truth.

The philosophical dilemma was perhaps not the only reason or even the main reason Wang Guowei gave up philosophy. China did not have educational or research institutions for the study of Western thought at the time. Wang Guowei had been able to study Western philosophy only because of Luo Zhenyu's patronage. It was Luo Zhenyu who sponsored his education in the Eastern Languages Society and who procured various positions for him that enabled him to continue scholarly pursuits. Luo Zhenyu's disapproval may have affected Wang Guowei's decision in regard to Western philosophy.

Luo Zhenyu remembered an anecdote that occurred soon after the 1911 Revolution when he and Wang Guowei had gone into a self-exile in Japan. In a conversation between them, Luo Zhenyu blamed Western philosophy for what had happened in China:

> Many Western philosophers made their arguments in a way similar to non-Confucian philosophers of the Zhou and Qin period. Some of these doctrines such as that of Nietzsche disparage benevolence and righteousness, hold modesty in contempt, and renounce the virtue of self-restraint. They even hope to create a new culture to replace the old one.* Many evils have resulted from this. Nowadays there are more opinions floating around than ever before. To keep alive the three-thousand-year tradition of Confucianism, one must repudiate these wrong views and return to Confucian classics.

Luo Zhenyu remembered Wang Guowei's response:

> Upon hearing these words, Wang Guowei trembled. He regretted that what he had learned before was not pure knowledge. Thereupon he took more than a hundred copies of his *Jin An Collection* [the collection of Wang Guowei's essays, including all his writings on Western philosophy] from his trunk and burned them all.²⁴

Luo Zhenyu did not say whether this incidence was the first occasion when he expressed his disapproval of Western philosophy. Wang Guowei may already have been under his pressure for a few years. Otherwise it would have been difficult to explain why, after writing "Schopenhauer and

---

* Wang Guowei wrote in his "Nietzsche and Schopenhauer," that both Schopenhauer and Nietzsche tried replace the old culture with a new one.

Nietzsche," he stopped mentioning Nietzsche's name, even when he was obviously referring to his ideas.

Wang Guowei had given up philosophy and literature once and for all. His voluminous writings since 1911 deal only with subjects such as inscriptions on oracle bones, genealogy of royal families in remote legendary times, ancient writings discovered in caves and deserts, and archaic institutions and customs. For him Western philosophy had become a faded memory. Kano Naoki, a Japanese scholar who knew him well, recollected:

> During our conversations, whenever I mentioned Western philosophy, Mr. Wang would always smile bitterly and say that he did not understand the subject.[25]

Where did Wang Guowei's bitterness come from? Could it be that he simply felt that Western philosophy had failed to supply him a vision that was both believable and lovable? Or was it caused by the memory of some traumatic incidents between him and Luo Zhenyu such as the aforementioned one? In any case, the very fact that the most promising student, if not the only promising student, of Western philosophy in the beginning of the twentieth century had turned away from Western philosophy is symptomatic of an age when China was far from being prepared to appreciate Western ideas on the philosophical level.

In 1927, after one and a half decades of devoted work in antiquarian studies, Wang Guowei committed suicide, an event that baffled his biographers. Some attributed it to Wang Guowei's loyalist sentiments: he was shocked at the news that the abdicated Qing emperor was mistreated by a military strongman and that some conservative scholars were killed by revolutionary armies. Others pointed to the increased tension between Wang Guowei and Luo Zhenyu, now in-laws through the marriage of their children. But could Wang Guowei's personal crisis have been aggravated by a disillusionment with the scholarly pursuits he had engaged in for so long? If factual certainty in China's antiquity was as "believable" as Nietzsche's philosophy, was it really any more "lovable"? Perhaps Wang Guowei had been consumed by an "ennui" that he had referred to many years ago in his essay on hobbies, and his life could have been saved by a more invigorating "active suffering."[26]

Notes

[1] Wang Guowei, *Complete Works of Wang Guowei* [《王觀堂先生全集》] (Taipei: Wenhua Press, 1968), vol. 5, 1737-1738.

[2] "The Teachings of Kant—the Greatest Philosopher in Modern Times," (《近世第一大哲康德之學說》) in Liang Qichao, *Collected Works*, vol. 5, issue 13, 49-60.

[3] Wang Guowei, "Random Thoughts on Education," from *Complete Works*, 103-108.

[4] *Ibid.*

[5] Masaaki Kosaka, ed., *Japanese Thought in the Meiji Era*, translated and adopted by David Abosch (Tokyo: Pan-Pacific Press, 1958), 358-360.

[6] Wang Guowei, *Complete Works*, 1824.

[7] Joey Bonner, *Wang Kuo-wei: an Intellectual History* (Cambridge, Mass: Harvard University Press, 1986), 20.

[8] Wang Guowei, *Complete Works*, 1658

[9] *Ibid.*, 1659-1661. Schopenhauer's argument can be found in his *The World As Will and Idea*, London: Routledge & Paul Ltd., 1883 (Ninth impression, 1950), Book 4, 491-492.

[10] Wang Guowei, "Schopenhauer's Philosophy and his Theory of Education," in *Complete Works*, vol. 5, 1596-1628.

[11] Wang Guowei, *Complete Works*, vol. 5, 1547, 1672.

[12] Wilhelm Windelband, *A History of Philosophy*, trans. by James H. Tufts (New York: Macmillan Company, 1914, a reprint of the 1901 edition which was based on the second German Edition), p. 677.

[13] Wang, *Complete Works*, vol. 5, 1690-1691.

[14] *Ibid.*, 1691-1693.

[15] *Ibid.*, 1693-1695.

[16] *Ibid.*

[17] *Ibid.* The fable is from *Lie Zi*, a fourth century B.C. book; for English translation see *The Book of Lieh-tzu*, trans. by A. C. (Angus Charles) Graham, (London: Murray, 1961).

[18] Wang Guowei, *Complete Works*, 1698-1695

[19] Wang Guowei, "On the Heavenly Duty of Philosophers and Artists," in *Complete Works*, vol. 5, 1748-1752; and varius versions of his *Reviews of the Ci form of Poems* [《人間詞話》].

[20] Wang Guowei, *Complete Works*, vol. 5, 1795-1803.

[21] *Ibid.*, 1795-1796.

²² This translation is based on Fung Yu-lan, *A Short History of Chinese Philosophy*, trans. Derk Bodde, (New York: The Free Press, A Division of Macmillan Publishing Co., 1966), 327.
²³ Wang Guowei referred to "Nietzsche's positivism" in his writing, see *Complete Works*, vol. 5, 1693-1695; also see p. 21 of the current book.
²⁴ Luo Zhenyu, "A Biography of Wang Guowei from Haining," [《羅振玉, 海甯王忠愨公傳》] in Wang Guowei, *Complete Works*, vol. 16, 7019-7022.
²⁵ Bonner, 160.
²⁶ Refer to p. 23.

CHAPTER 3

Nietzsche and the "New Culture"

Between 1915 and the early 1920s there was a burst of energy and vitality on China's intellectual stage. As it became obvious that the 1911 Revolution had failed to improve China's domestic situation and its international standing, many intellectuals, especially those had lived and studied in Western countries or in Japan, began to suspect that there was something fundamentally wrong with China's culture and they should create a "new culture" to replaced it. All of a sudden magazines, newspapers and booklets that criticized things Chinese and promoted Western values, ideas, practices, and institutions flourished. This is the phenomenon usually referred to as the New Culture Movement.*

The New Culture Movement was not an organized movement. It was, however, inseparably associated with a few prominent writers and scholars who were its spiritual leaders. To various degrees, all these leading figures were drawn to Nietzsche at some point of their lives and their comments on Nietzsche offer us an unusual opportunity to comprehend their mind-set and the movement to which they belonged.

The launching of the journal *New Youth* in 1915 heralded the New Culture Movement. In the journal's first issue, its founder Chen Duxiu, a flamboyant writer and political activist returning from France, made a passionate appeal to Chinese youth, asking them to be "independent, not

---

* The New Culture Movement has alternatively been referred to as the May Fourth Movement. There have also been attempts to make distinctions between the two phrases. The current book will use "the New Culture Movement" in a broader sense.

servile," "progressive, not conservative," "active, not passive," "cosmopolitan, not isolationist," "utilitarian, not formalistic," "scientific, not indulging in imagination." He invoked Nietzsche to underline the importance of independence:

> All men are equal. Everyone is entitled to be independent. He has absolutely no right to enslave others nor is he obliged to be servile to others.... The great German philosopher Nietzsche made distinctions between two moralities: the morality that demonstrates independence and courage is "master morality"; the morality that shows humility and docility is "slave morality"[1]

Here the reduction of two philosophical concepts into mere personal attributes reveals the Chen Duxiu's ignorance of Nietzsche's genealogy of morals. Actually Chen Duxiu was not talking about philosophy at all. Since the early 1900s calling their countrymen "slaves" had been a rhetoric used by Chinese reformers and revolutionaries alike. They used it to vent their frustration at people's political apathy.* Chen Duxiu himself was among the first Chinese to use such rhetoric. His essay "A Warning to Slaves," written in 1903 includes the following comment:

> Due to the influences of three thousand years of slave history, of thousands of years of slave customs, of numerous generations of slave education, and of many slave philosophies, the Chinese are born slaves. All these influences, having continued from generation to generation, developed into a [slave-] nature.[2]

Also in 1903, in retelling the story of Victor Hugo's *Les Misérables*, Chen Duxiu (and Su Manshu) took the liberty to add to the novel a fictional character—Nan De [男德, meaning "masculine virtue"] who addressed his French compatriots with the following words:

> The Confucian teachings for the slaves are venerated only by the submissive Chinese race. Are we, noble citizens of France, also going to listen to such rubbish?[3]

Obviously Chen Duxiu was unable to distinguish between rhetoric and philosophy. He must have mistaken Nietzsche for a comrade when he learned that Nietzsche also disapproved of "slave morality."

---

* Liang Qichao was among the first to use such rhetoric, see p. 10 of the current book. Another example was Zou Rong (Tsou Jung), a revolutionary pamphleteer, see *The Revolutionary Army: A Chinese Nationalist Tract of 1903*, trans. by John Lust (The Hague, 1968).

It is difficult to pinpoint the sources from which Chen Duxiu had learned about Nietzsche. Since he lived in Japan from 1907 to 1909, he may have witnessed the warm reception the Japanese had accorded Nietzsche. His own admiration for the German philosophy was so great that he even invoked him to vindicate his own Francophile sentiment:

> When France was defeated by Germany, the great German philosopher Nietzsche warned, "We Germans must not be complacent because of this victory. The creative genius of the French is superior to our imitation culture."[4]

The quoted sentence was a paraphrase of one passage from Nietzsche's article "David Strauss, the Confessor and the Writer" in *Untimely Meditations*.[5] Chen Duxiu had so much simplified Nietzsche's ideas that he did not seem to understand Nietzsche's intention at all.

Chen Duxiu's knowledge of Nietzsche and Western philosophy in general was minimal. All he knew about the West was a vague idea of individualism:

> Western nations, from ancient times to the present, have been thoroughly individualistic. Britain and the US are individualistic, so are France and Germany. Nietzsche was individualistic, so was Kant. The goal of all ethics, morality, politics and laws, the aspirations of the society, and the mission of the state, all point to individual freedom, individual rights and happiness.[6]

It was such a childish notion of individualism that encouraged Chen Duxiu and other Chinese writers to criticize China for its alleged lack of individualism.

Chen Duxiu had learned a little more about the West over the next two years. In a speech delivered in 1917, he divided moral doctrines into three schools. Two of the three were from the West: individualist egoism and socialist altruism. The former originated from the Greco-Roman tradition and, in modern times, had undergone a transformation from the Darwinian theory of the struggle for survival to Nietzsche's theory of superman, and thence to German militarism. The latter grew out of the Christian tradition and was now championed by Tolstoi. Beside the two Western moral schools, there was a third—the Chinese Confucian morality, neither egoistic nor altruistic, neither individualist nor socialist, but merely a "slave morality" based on a "patriarchal system."[7]

What Chen Duxiu referred to as two Western moral schools turned out to be nothing particularly Western. When he talked about Western socialist altruist tradition, he had in mind Buddhism and Mohist "universal love" [兼愛]. He criticized the Mohists for being "too one-sided" in calling for "sacrificing oneself for others." He contended that even Buddhism, the "ultimate altruism," was a kind of egoism, for a Buddhist was after all concerned with his own deliverance from suffering. When he talked about Western individualist egoism, he had in mind Chinese philosopher Yang Zhu's idea of "for oneself" [爲我]. He did not distinguish between Nietzsche and Yang Zhu and used both merely as symbols of an "individualist egoism":

> While the teaching of Yang Zhu and Nietzsche reveals the truth of life, if it is followed to its extreme, how can any civilized and complex society such as ours sustain itself?*⁸

Chen Duxiu was not completely satisfied with the two "Western" moral schools. In his view an ideal solution was to broaden egoism, to extend it to a community, a nation, and mankind. There is an irony in Chen Duxiu's attitude toward Confucianism. While giving both "Western" moral schools some credit, he regarded Confucianism as completely worthless. If anyone was still attached to it, Chen Duxiu remarked, he simply "has not rid himself of slavishness and does not have the courage to live as a citizen." In reality his criticism of the two "Western" moral traditions is an exact copy of Confucian criticism of Mo Di and Yang Zhu. Confucius stood above the debate between the Mohists and the Yang Zhu School and he refused to choose between the interest of the individual and that of society. The "principle of extending" [恕道] is a classical Confucian solution to the debate. Thus while Chen Duxiu thought he was commenting on two Western moral traditions, he was actually reviewing an ancient philosophical dialogue within China's own intellectual tradition from a purely Confucian point of view.

Chen Duxiu's failure to recognize his own identity and his tendency to use Nietzsche or other Western thinkers as symbols to express his own Chinese ideas came partly from a social Darwinist prejudice. A nation that was backward economically and militarily must have inferior ideas and moral traditions, and vice versa. Out of the same prejudice he viewed the First World War as testing ground for what he thought as the two Western moral principles. And he believed that the post-war world would be

---

* Mo Di (c. 470 B.C. — c. 391 B.C.) was the founder of the Mohist School. His teachings were recorded in the book *Mo Zi*. Yang Zhu (430 B.C. — c. 360 B.C.) was the founder of the Yang Zhu school. His own writings have been lost, but some of his ideas are known to us through the words of his critics.

dominated by the moral principle of the winning side. Since he believed that France and the United States stood for democracy, justice and peace, he looked forward to the Allied victory with great expectation.

The Paris Peace Conference disillusioned him. In February he was shocked at the exclusion of Belgium from important negotiations and the monopoly of the peace process by the Five Powers. He was also outraged by the suppression of the Spartacists in Germany by Kaiser's supporters.[9] Eventually he came to the conclusion that the Western powers, instead of representing the "altruist moral school" as he had believed, were also part of the "individualist egoist" tradition.

Now Chen Duxiu was no longer even-handed toward the two "Western" moral schools. He became critical of the one which he had associated with Nietzsche and in favor of the other. He commented:

> I believe that Christianity is a religion of love. As long as we don't accept Nietzsche's rejection of love among men, we should not draw the conclusion that Christianity is finished. After all, the essence of Christianity is love and faith, all others are secondary.[10]

Here, just as in the cases discussed earlier, Chen Duxiu used Christianity and Nietzsche merely as symbols or labels of some general values. All he wanted to express was that he preferred an international order based on morality to the one based purely on geopolitical considerations.

Chen Duxiu's new perception of "Western" moral traditions did not make him less critical of the Chinese one which he had previously condemned for its alleged lack of individualism. Instead, he now attacked the Chinese tradition from a different angle—asserting that there was an "absence of pure aesthetic and religious sentiments in the fountainhead of the Chinese culture."[11]

In a certain sense Chen Duxiu did undergo a religious conversion in early 1919, though not a Christian one. Having long lost faith in China's own traditions and recently disillusioned with the capitalist West, he was drawn to Bolshevik Russia which he now believed to embody the "Western" altruist tradition. His criticism of "Western" individualism was simultaneious with his adoption of Marxist rhetoric in his writings. He wrote, for example:

> International power politics, political injustice, the vices of private property, class inequality, and various laws and moralities that are irrational and inappropriate for a spontaneous life... are the bitter fruits of the dark side of our nature, of our greed, cruelty, and selfishness, of qualities that are no different

from other animals.[12]

Such comments, while revealing a mere superficial acquaintance with Marxism on the part of Chen Duxiu, illustrate how well the Marxist outlook could fit the mindset of intellectuals like him.

Since 1919 Chen Duxiu and many other Chinese intellectuals began to discuss and advocate Marxism. *New Youth*, the journal that had served as the most important forum of the New Culture Movement since 1915, was gradually turned into a tribune for Marxist writers. When the Chinese Communist Party was founded by Chen Duxiu and his comrades in 1921, *New Youth* became the new party's organ.

Chen Duxiu's life was heroic and tragic. He was made a scapegoat by the Comintern for the setback of the Chinese communist movement in 1927 and removed from his position as the CCP's general secretary.* Two years later he was expelled from the party for his connection with the Trotskyites. Then he was thrown into jail by the GMD for being a communist and, at the same time, attacked by his former comrades for betraying communism. In his later years he denounced Stalinist totalitarianism and advocated democratic socialism. When the Second World War was touched off by the Nazi invasion of Poland, he criticized both the Stalinists and the Trotskyites for not seeking an alliance with the West, warning that mankind would descend into a dark age for centuries if Nazism were allowed to prevail. He died in May 27, 1942 before he could witness the Allied victory.

Li Dazhao [1889–1905] was another leading figure in the era of the New Culture. After returning to China from Japan in the summer of 1916, he launched the newspaper *Morning Bell* to propagate new ideas. He wrote two short biographies in succession, one about Tolstoi, published on August 20, the other about Nietzsche, one August 22. He praised Tolstoi for the moral values he stood for, especially his compassion for the downtrodden peasants. About Nietzsche, he gave the following description:

> Nietzsche was a man who was determined to live an authentic life based upon his needs and convictions. He urged the weak to gain strength and the imperfect to seek perfection. He led a life that was tragic, honest, and profound. To liberate and uplift human nature he did not flinch from fighting a hundred battles and he showed great valor in combat. He made penetrating observations about his own mind and life. He relentlessly criticized the social status quo. He took upon

---

* The CCP and the GMD stand for the Chinese Communist Party and the Nationalist Party (Guomindang).

himself to study and address the weakness of human nature and the flaws of civilization. He was certainly a man who loved himself, society, and civilization, and who embraced life with passion.

Nietzsche's thought had gone through three changes. At first he was influenced by Schopenhauer and Wagner and believed that life existed only for the sake of art. Then, influenced by Paul Rée, he shifted his focus to intellect. Later combining art and intellect and relying on man's will and creativity, he gave individualism a foundation. He fiercely attacked nineteenth century philistinism and materialism. He believed that life's true meaning tends to be obscured by empty talks in the name of religion, morality, fraternity and humanism and men will be trapped in sickness and vices as long as they keep wearing a mask of hypocrisy and always compromise and appease. In order to guide modern civilization into the realm of a new idealism, Nietzsche promoted a superman philosophy, called for heroism, glorified the joy of power, exalted great characters, and preached the gospel of war. His teaching is capable of invigorating the degenerate and the decadent. Since our nation is extremely formalistic and conformist, and handicapped by a slave morality, his teaching will prove effective in uplifting the spirit of our youth and boosting our people's courage.[13]

By our standard such an introduction seems inadequate and problematic. It touches upon many aspects of Nietzsche's philosophy but elaborates on none. The Nietzsche portrayed in it merely represents certain general values and personal attributes instead of a thinker with unique ideas. The short biography was obviously based on some secondary sources, or maybe just from an encyclopedia entry. Yet this short introduction was the only available biographical sketch of Nietzsche in China at the time and its author seemed to be more sophisticated and disciplined in thinking than Chen Duxiu.

While neither Chen Duxiu nor Li Dazhao discussed Nietzsche and Tolstoi on philosophical terms, their approaches were different. Chen Duxiu used Nietzsche and Tolstoi as symbols to dramatize what he considered to be the two conflicting "Western" moral schools. Li Dazhao set up Nietzsche and Tolstoi as two role models for himself and for Chinese youth, whose personal qualities were different but similarly worth emulating. Just as in the case of Chen Duxiu, there was something very Chinese in Li Dazhao's attitude toward Western thinkers. The Chinese had always treated their ancient philosophers as role models rather than as mere individuals with good ideas.

There is no evidence that Li Dazhao had a lasting interest in either Tolstoi or Nietzsche. When the Bolshevik Revolution broke out in Russia,

Li Dazhao immediately saw it as an embodiment of the values that he had believed to be represented by Tolstoi and Nietzsche, that is, a combination of universal love, liberation of labor and farmers, and a heroic revolt against oppression and injustice and against international power politics. He was one of the first Chinese to welcome the Russian Bolshevik Revolution and to introduce its ideas to Chinese readers. He was one of the cofounders of the Chinese Communist Party.

Through studying Marxist theory and Western historical theory in general, Li Dazhao had gradually acquired in-depth knowledge on certain aspects of Western thought. He probably was the best theorist the CCP had in its early years. His interpretation of Marxism was undogmatic, ingenious and thorough. Li Dazhao had long left his youthful fancies about Nietzsche and Tolstoi behind. But in his life he had always aspired after those fine qualities that he attributed to Nietzsche and Tolstoi in his 1916 biographies.

Guo Moruo was studying medicine in Japan in 1919. When some poems he sent back to China were published, he became a nationally known poet overnight. He wrote many more poems since then. He sang of love's joy and sorrow, of the nature's beauty, of individual freedom, and of the mysterious power of art. He also sang the praise of rebels and revolutionaries. In his "Ode to Bandits," a poem he wrote at the end of 1919 to extol all kinds of "bandits," Nietzsche was among the "bandits of intellectual revolutions":

> Hail to Copernicus, who dared to advocate (*sic*) the solar system and to differ from sacred texts and conventions!
>
> Hail to Darwin, the monster who vilified human ancestry by insisting on the common origin of men and apes!
>
> Hail to Nietzsche, who advocated the Superman philosophy, and blasphemed God and smashed the idols!
>
> All bandits of intellectual revolution, from the West, the East, the North and the South, from the past, the present and the future,
>
> May you live forever!

One should not assume that Guo Moruo knew much about any of the eighteen "bandits" mentioned in the poem. He simply enjoyed rattling off these big names and feeling himself at one with them in a romantic rebellion. His reference to Nietzsche does not necessarily imply he had a special interest in the German philosopher at the time.[14]

Guo Moruo became serious about Nietzsche in 1923 when he began to translate *Thus Spoke Zarathustra*. The translation appeared in installments in *Creation Weekly*, a journal he launched in May of 1923. The role of Nietzsche was implied in a poem Guo Moruo dedicated to the journal:

God, you are the first creator,

I call on your name, not to glorify you,

Ancient poets said that you took only seven days to create the world.

You created light on the first day,

You created the firmament that divided water on the second day;

you created the earth and oceans on the third day,

And upon the earth, you created vegetables and fruit trees;

You created the sun, the moon and the stars on the fourth day;

You created swimming fish and flying birds on the fifth day;

You created beasts, insects, and us, mankind, on the sixth day;

But all of a sudden, on the seventh day, you became lazy and negligent.

God, if you had really created the world in such a manner,

You must have done a shoddy work in creating us, mankind,

Your last product, your worst product, doomed to be classified

Eternally along with insects and beasts.

All the selfishness, all the internecine killing, and all the ignorance, and indolence of mankind resulted from your carelessness and negligence.

Why did you end work in such a hurry on the seventh day, without polishing your half-finished work?

God, we are not satisfied with such a life full of defects,

We are going to create ourselves from scratch,

And our project will start from the seventh day,

The day you became careless and negligent. [15]

It seems that the poet was going to play the role of a better God than God and to recreate mankind. Apparently feeling himself not up to such a task, he called in Nietzsche to help create a better mankind—the superman. From May 1923 on, one chapter after another, the Chinese translation of *Thus Spoke Zarathustra* appeared in *Creation Weekly* almost every week. By the end of the year, the book's first part had been all translated and published.

Guo Moruo had planned to translate *Thus Spoke Zarathustra* in its entirety. But after completing the first four sections of the book's second part, he abandoned the plan in February 1924. Thirty years later, in 1958, he gave an explanation of why he stopped translating the book: "The revolution was gathering strength in China. It drew my attention from the sky to the earth and distanced me from Nietzsche." He also claimed that his discontinuance of the translation meant his "rejection of Nietzsche."[16]

The "revolution" in question refers to the new level of political activism in China in 1923-1924 when the Nationalists and the Communists formed the "United Front" under the auspices of the Comintern. Guo Moruo's biographical records show that he did not abandon Nietzsche to join the revolution. Guo Moruo had a domestic crisis at the time he stopped translating *Thus Spoke Zarathustra*. Since his return to China in April 1923, Tomiko, his Japanese wife, had always implored him to practice medicine instead of pursuing a literary career. She and their three children did not know a word of Chinese and, living in Shanghai, they missed the outdoor environment they used to enjoy in Japan. After many quarrels, she departed for Japan with the children on February 17, leaving Guo Moruo in great anxiety. The last section of *Thus Spoke Zarathustra* he was able to finish was published in the thirty-ninth issue of *Creation Weekly* on February 3, 1924. On April 1 Guo Moruo left China to join his wife and children, swearing that he would never again set foot on Chinese soil.[17] He was not telling the truth when he said he was drawn away from Nietzsche by "the revolution." It was in 1926 that he returned to China to join the Northern Expedition, leaving his wife and children behind in Japan. By then the translation project had long been a history.

Thus when, in 1958, he tried to explain why he stopped translating *Thus Spoke Zarathustra* more than thirty years ago, there was obviously a lapse of memory regarding the sequence of events. However, his referring to Nietzsche's philosophy as something in the sky reveals the real cause of his failure to finish the translation—Nietzsche was too difficult for him.

Since he began to translate *Thus Spoke Zarathustra*, he was often asked one question—"What does Zarathustra mean after all?" After finishing the first part of *Thus Spoke Zarathustra*, he wrote an essay "Aphorism and Self-reliance" as a response. He explained that he translated the book with the hope that "readers will be enticed to read the original." He warned that the readers should not trust his translation which, after all, was but an interpretation. He did not give the least hint of how he understood Zarathustra. The excuse is suggested by the essay's title: Aphorisms defies interpretation and readers have to rely on themselves. As an author known for his eloquence on almost any subject, his modesty in regard to *Thus Spoke Zarathustra* shows how much he had been bewildered by the book.

Even without the family crisis, it is doubtful if he could ever have finished the translation. He was able to complete the first part because it has a clear story line. He must have found the second part more difficult to understand. He inappropriately translated the section "On the Pitying" ("Von den Mitleidigen") as "On Philanthropists." He delivered the next section "On Priests" much later than usual, with four issues of *Creation Weekly* between. And he stopped at "On the Virtuous," the fifth section of Part Two. This is one of the most fascinating sections of *Thus Spoke Zarathustra*, in which Nietzsche tried to unveil the hidden psychological mechanisms of what is usually called virtue. Nietzsche's alternative to the "virtuous" is his motto that "your self be in your deeds as the mother is in her child." Such ideas, if not understood, cannot possibly be put into words in a different language.

Judging from the whole body of his writings, one has to conclude that Guo Moruo was at his best when dealing with social and political philosophies but weak in moral philosophy and psychology. The failure to proceed with the translation must have caused a feeling of inferiority and futility, as reflected in Guo Moruo's four biographical short stories written in February and March of 1924. It even made him suspect his talent as a creative writer.[18]

Once in Japan with his wife and children, Guo Moruo tried to continue studying medicine but was unable to obtain financial support from the Chinese government. Then, in May and June, he read and translated Kawakami Hajime's *Social Organization and Social Revolution*, an introductory book on Marxism and Leninism. The book's impact on him was great:

> It [the book] has awakened me from my semi-somnolent status. It has stopped

me from wavering at crossroads. It has rescued me from the shadow of death. I am deeply grateful to the author and profoundly grateful to Marx and Lenin.... The thing which has amazed me the most in translating this book is the fact that men like Lenin and Trotsky, whom we have been accustomed to regard as little more than desperadoes, have such subtle minds and are such dedicated scholars.[19]

So it was from the "subtle minds" of Lenin and Trotsky that Guo Moruo had regained the confidence he had lost to Nietzsche.

Marxism was not new to Guo Moruo. As early as May 1923 when he launched the magazine *Creation Weekly*, Guo Moruo's interest in Nietzsche was already mixed with an excitement over communism.[20] His translation of Zarathustra often appeared side by side with his essays full of Marxist jargons in the magazine. He needed Nietzsche in his effort to create a better mankind (that, in his view, was what Nietzsche meant by superman) and he needed Marx to simulate a battle against capitalism. His essays and his incomplete translation in the magazine demonstrate beyond doubt that he understood neither Nietzsche nor Marx at the time. Guo Moruo, however, had one superior quality that was missing in Liang Qichao or Chen Duxiu: he was willing to read and translate *Thus Spoke Zarathustra* and Kawakami Hajime's book. In the process he was able to discover his weakness and his strength.

Since Guo Moruo was rescued by Kawakami Hajime from his humiliating experience with Nietzsche, he considered himself a Marxist. In the late 1920s and the 1930s, he promoted proletarian literature and was a central figure in the left-wing literary movement. He applied Marxism to the study of Chinese history and philosophy and established himself as a leading Marxist scholar. Guo Moruo's turning to Marxism did not constitute, as he claimed in 1958, a "rejection" of Nietzsche. Philosophically he had never understood Nietzsche and, hence, had nothing to reject. He admired Nietzsche as a literary genius and continued to respect him after his conversion to Marxism. When his poem "Ode to the Bandits" was reprinted in 1928, the name of Nietzsche was still among the eighteen "bandits," while Bertrand Russell and Francis Galton, two "bandits of social revolution," were replaced by Karl Marx and Friedrich Engels.[21] In the early 1940s when he condemned the political use of Nietzsche by the Chinese right, he still referred to Nietzsche as a "great philosopher."

Of the leading intellectuals in the Era of New Culture, Hu Shih was one of the few who did not turn to Marxism. The three writers discussed so far in the current chapter had one thing in common: they had no training in social theories before their contact with Marxism. In contrast, Hu Shih had completed a Ph.D. program under John Dewey when he returned to China in 1917 and he shared with his mentor a faith in gradualist reforms. A regular contributor to Chen Duxiu's journal *New Youth*, Hu Shih advocated a new literature that would be more accessible and relevant to common people and promoted the use of vernacular Chinese instead of classical Chinese as the main form of writing. Hu Shih was not attracted to the Bolshevik revolution. In a friendly debate with Li Dazhao about "isms and issues," Hu Shih rejected the idea that China could be transformed overnight by any revolutionary "ism" and insisted on the importance of studying and solving individual issues confronting China.

Hu Shih had never been a fan of Nietzsche. But by 1919 Nietzsche had become such a powerful symbol in China that even Hu Shih was carried away. In an article entitled "The Meaning of New Thinking," he characterized the essence of "new thinking" as an "attitude of evaluation," which, he explained, meant that one must look into everything from new perspectives, in order to identify its advantages and disadvantages,

> Nietzsche said that our time is an age of "revaluation of all values." "Revaluation of all values" is the best interpretation of the attitude of evaluation. In previous ages, the smaller a woman's feet were, the prettier they were thought to be. Now we no longer think foot-binding pretty, on the contrary, we consider the custom to be cruel and inhuman.[22]

Here the reference to Nietzsche added nothing to Hu Shih's common sense approach. After all one does not need Nietzsche's "revaluation of all values" to condemn foot-binding. Affected by a fad of his time, Hu Shih made the mistake of explaining a simple concept with a complicated one which he did not fully understand.

Chen Duxiu, Li Dazhao, Guo Moruo and Hu Shih were leading figures of the New Culture Movement. Their references to Nietzsche were symptomatic of an era when China still was in the process of intellectual maturation. Although some of them began to grasp Western social and political theories, in the area of philosophy, they had not gone beyond the stage of symbol-juggling.

Notes

[1] Chen Duxiu, "To Youth," *New Youth*, vol. no. 1 (1915). The translation is based on Ssu-yu Teng, *China's Response to the West*, 239-251.

[2] The article appeared in *Citizens' Daily*, a revolutionary journal edited by Chen Duxiu. See Chen Wanxiong, *Chen Duxiu before the New Cultural Movement, 1879-1915* (Hong Kong: Hong Kong Chinese University Press, 1979), 116.

[3] The article appeared in *Citizens' Daily*, a revolutionary journal edited by Chen Duxiu. See Chen Wanxiong, *Chen Duxiu Before the New Cultural Movement, 1879-1915* (Hong Kong: Hong Kong Chinese University Press, 1979), 119.

[4] Chen Duxiu, "The French Nation and Modern Civilization," [法蘭西民族與近世文明] in *Selected Writings of Chen Duxiu* (Beijing: Sanlian Books, 1984) [北京，三聯書店，《陳獨秀文章選編》], 79-81. Originally published in *New Youth*, vol. 1, no. 1 (Sept. 15, 1915). About the fact that Chen Duxiu visited Japan, instead of France, see Lee Feigon, *Chen Duxiu: Founder of the Chinese Communist Party*, Princeton University Press, 1983, 82-83.

[5] Nietzsche, Friedrich Wilhelm. *Untimely Meditations*. (Cambridge/New York: Cambridge University Press, 1983), 6.

[6] Chen Duxiu, "The Differences in the Basic Ideas of Western and Eastern Nations," [東西民族根本思想之差異] in *Selected Writings*, 97-100. Originally published in *New Youth*, vol. 1, no. 4 (December 15, 1915).

[7] Chen Duxiu, "The Definition of Morality and Schools of Moral Teachings," [道德之概念及其學說派別] in *Selected Writing*, 194-195. Originally published in *New Youth*, vol. 3, no. 3, (March 17, 1917).

[8] *Ibid.* and Chen Duxiu, "The Essence of Life," [人生眞意] in *Selected Writings*, 239-240. Originally published in *New Youth*, vol. 4, no. 2, (February 15, 1918). Chen Duxiu seemed to share the same feeling with Wang Guowei that Nietzsche's philosophy was believable but not lovable. Cf. p. 23.

[9] Chen Duxiu, "Where Is Justice?" [公理何在] in *Selected Writings*, 342. Originally published in *Maizhou Pinglun*, [每周評論] no. 7. (February 2, 1919).

[10] Chen Duxiu, "Christianity and the Chinese," [基督教與中國人] in *Selected Writings*, 482-489. Originally published in *New Youth*, vol. 7, no. 3, (February 1, 1920).

[11] *Ibid.*

[12] Chen Duxiu, "What Shall We Do?" [我們應該怎樣？] in *Selected Writings*, p. 380. Originally published in *New Youth*, vol.6, no. 4, (April 15, 1919).

[13] Li Dazhao, "An Introduction to Leo Tolstoi," [介紹哲人托爾斯泰] in *Selected Writings of Li Dazhao* (Beijing: People's Press, 1984), vol. 1, 186-187, Originally published in the *Morning Bell*, August 20, 1916; "An Introduction to Friedrich Nietzsche," [介紹哲人尼采] in *Selected Writings*, vol. 1. 188-189, Originally published in *Morning Bell*, August 22, 1916.

[14] David Tod Roy, *Kuo Mo-Jo: The Early Years*. (Cambridge, Massachusetts: Harvard University Press, 1971), 69.

[15] Zhao Jiabi, *Grand Series of the Chinese New Literature*, vol. 10, 103–104.
[16] Gong Nianzhai and Fang Rennian, *A Biography of Guo Moruo* [龔濟之，方年仁，《郭沫若年譜》] (Tianjin: Tianjin People's Press, 1982), 124.
[17] Roy, 131.
[18] Roy, 156–157.
[19] based on (Translated by Roy, p. 159).
[20] One scholar observed that there was a "marked shift of emphasis" in his writings when he launched *Creation Weekly*, referring to his interest in the communist movement. Roy, 147.
[21] Guo Moruo, *Complete Works of Guo Moruo*, Literature Series (Beijing: People's Literature Press, 1982), vol. 1, 116.
[22] Hu Shih, "The Meaning of the New Thought," [新思潮的意義，《胡適文存》第一集] in *Writings of Hu Shih*, (Shanghai: Ya Dong Tu Shu Guan, 1930), vol. 1, pp. 728-729.

CHAPTER 4

Lu Xun:

A "Nietzschean Man of Strength"

In the literary history of twentieth-century China, no one has been more frequently referred to as a Nietzschean writer than Lu Xun. Since the 1920s, Lu Xun has been frivolously called "China's Nietzsche" by his admirers and detractors alike. His essays and short stories have been seen as representing Nietzsche's ideas. As late as the 1980s he was still quoted as an authority on Nietzsche. Lu Xun himself could not be held responsible for such perceptions: he had never pretended to be an expert on Nietzsche and on more than one occasion he acknowledged his ignorance of Nietzsche's philosophy.

For a long time scholars have been trying to decide on such issues as how much Lu Xun was influenced by Nietzsche at various stages of his life, how Nietzsche's influence interacted with other influences, and whether or when Lu Xun turned away from Nietzsche to Bolshevism. Their efforts have brought new perspectives and insights to the study of Lu Xun. One basic question, however, has yet to be adequately answered: what exactly did Nietzsche mean to Lu Xun?

Lu Xun was born into a well-to-do gentry family in 1881 in Shaoxing, Zhejiang province.[1] Although his father was unable to advance any further than the first level of civil service examinations, his grandfather had served senior positions in the royal government in Beijing. Lu Xun would have grown up in a protected environment, had he not been forced to face harsh realities due to family vicissitudes. In 1893, when he was twelve years old, his grandfather, accused of corruption, was sentenced to death with a reprieve by an imperial decree. Although the sentence was eventually repealed and his grandfather released, the family was impoverished in tending the case. As if the legal entanglement was not enough, his father fell ill in 1894. Lu Xun had to go to pawn shops and drugstores almost daily, to get money and buy medicine for his father, whose condition continued to deteriorate until he died three years later. Throughout these difficult years Lu Xun, a teenage boy, witnessed how his family was ill-treated by snobbish relatives and acquaintances. About these early experiences Lu Xun later wrote: "Anyone who tumbles from affluence into poverty will, on the way down, come to see the true face of the world."[2]

In 1898, the year of the Hundred Days Reform, Lu Xun left his home town for Nanjing. He first studied in the Jiangnan Navy School and then in the School of Railways and Mines, an affiliated institution of the Jiangnan Army School. After his graduation in 1902, he was sent by the provincial government to Japan for further studies. There he spent two years learning Japanese and in 1904 enrolled in a medical school in Sendai. Lu Xun had read Yan Fu's *On the Evolution of Heaven* and other Chinese reformers' writings. He viewed science and technology as means to make China stronger. He chose the medical profession because he "dreamed of going back [to China] after graduation to relieve patients like [his] father" and "to serve the army as a physician" in times of war.[3]

Life in medical school had not been an easy one for Lu Xun. In a letter to a friend written shortly after his arrival in Sendai, he complained about the fast learning pace and the school's over-reliance on rote memory. The only exciting event he mentioned in the letter was his reading a Chinese translation of *Uncle Tom's Cabin* by Harriet Beecher Stowe.[4] Despite his misgivings about the school, he worked hard to catch up on his studies. Lu Xun, the only Chinese in the city at the time, received generous help from Japanese professors in the school. He was especially grateful to Prof. Fujino, from whom he took four courses, and who kindly read and revised his class notes, even correcting his grammatical errors. Lu Xun managed to complete his first year's study with fair grades.

When the most difficult stage seemed to be over, two traumatic incidents occurred to him and made him rethink his choice of career. In the fall of 1905, some of his classmates who had failed in their final exams spread the rumor that Prof. Fujino had leaked test questions to Lu Xun. Lu Xun was hurt. Many years later, he was still bitter about this incident when he remembered it:

China is a weak nation. Therefore all Chinese are naturally incompetent. If a Chinese has scored more than 60 points in an exam, it couldn't be due to his effort, and there must be something fishy.[5]

The second incident was also related to China's status as an oppressed nation. Once Lu Xun and his classmates watched a documentary slide show about the Russo-Japanese War, a war fought mainly on Chinese soil. One slide showed a Chinese in the middle, bound up, with many other Chinese standing around, all physically strong, all with an expression of indifference. The script explained that the Chinese in the middle had spied for the Russians and was to be executed by the Japanese as a warning to other Chinese. As his Japanese classmates clapped and applauded, a thought flashed in his mind:

> Medicine is not a priority for China. All ignorant and cowardly people, no matter how healthy and strong they are, can serve as nothing but meaningless material to be pilloried or as bystanders. It may not be such a bad thing that such people get sick and die. The first priority should be to change their mentality.[6]

Lu Xun decided to take up literature which, he believed, was an effective tool to change the Chinese people's mentality.

In the spring of 1906 Lu Xun left the medical school and moved to Tokyo. One of his best friends remembered how he was surprised by Lu Xun who suddenly appeared in Tokyo:

> "I've quit the school", he [Lu Xun] told me.
>
> "Why?" I was surprised, wondering whether this was due to his caprice. "I thought you were interested in your studies? Why do you break off?"
>
> "Yes." He hesitated a little and finally said, "I've decided to study literature. The fools and evil fools of China, can they be cured by medicine?"
>
> We looked at each other, laughed with bitterness, because the fools and evil fools had often been the subjects of our discussion."[7]

Lu Xun did not go to a college to pursue a degree, nor did he begin a systematic study under a teacher's guidance. He simply waded through literary works on his own, without an overall plan. Nevertheless, with an eye for changing his countrymen's mentality, he was especially drawn to two groups of writers. The first group included a number of eastern and northern European authors, such as the Polish writer Henryk Sienkiewicz, the Czech writers Jan Neruda and Jaroslav Vrchlicky (pseudonym of Emil Frída), the Finnish writer Pietari Päivärinta, and the Hungarian writer

Sandor Petőfi. These were writers who urged their countrymen to resist foreign domination and fight for independence. The second group were writers critical of their own countries' social realities and their countrymen's mentality. Most of this group were from Russia, such as Nikolai Gogol, Anton Chekhov, and Leonid Andreyev, with one exception, Friedrich Nietzsche from Germany.[8]

Lu Xun's apprenticeship as writer resulted in five essays which he wrote between 1907 and 1908, all published in *Henan*, a Chinese magazine in Japan.* These essays touched upon a wide range of issues such as historical trends, international relations, changing values, functions of poets, literature, etc.. Although they were no more than a young man's bold attempts to understand the world and to establish his own identity, they contained themes that were to recur in his later writings.

Two of the five essays are about science. "The History of Man" (December 1907) is an introduction to Ernst Heinrich Haeckel's "biogenetic law." It shows that Lu Xun was still interested in science, particularly in the theory of evolution. The other essay, "A Lesson of the History of Science" (June 1908) focuses on the limitations of science. In the essay, Lu Xun surveyed the history of science in the West and concluded that knowledge must not be divorced from moral values and that thinkers and artists are just as important as scientists and engineers. He criticized his contemporary Chinese reformers for their preoccupation with technology while neglecting people's minds.[9]

The remaining essays deal with cultural issues and reveal Nietzsche's influence over young Lu Xun. In "On Cultural Extremes" (August 1908), Lu Xun argued that the West had been vacillating between "cultural extremes" throughout its history. People in each age had to correct certain "cultural extremes" they had inherited from the previous age. The very means they used to overcome these old "cultural extremes" would give rise to new "cultural extremes," which in their turn, had to be tackled by a later generation. For example, to fight obscurantism, poverty and autocracy—the

---

* Henan is the name of a province in China. It literally means "the South of the Yellow River." The dates of publication of the five essays are: December 1907 ("History of Man"), February and March 1908 ("On Satanic Poets"), June 1908 ("A Lesson of the History of Science"), August 1908 ("On Cultural Extremes"), December 1908 ("Rebuttal of Devious Talks"). The first four essays, however, were dated 1907 by the author.

"cultural extremes" of the medieval world, the modern West had acquired military power, scientific progress, economic prosperity, and political democracy. With the old "cultural extremes" gone, these new properties had become new "cultural extremes."

One of the modern "cultural extremes," Lu Xun believed, was democracy. Lu Xun considered democracy to be a noble ideal that carries with it the risk of neglecting men's "unique individuality" and "forcing individuals into uniformity." Another modern "cultural extreme" was an overemphasis on material progress at the expense of man's spiritual life. Lu Xun thought these two "cultural extremes" were especially dangerous to the Chinese who, he alleged, already had a tendency to be too "materialistic" and "intolerant of geniuses" in the past. He warned that if China was to import such "cultural extremes" from the West, it would have faired no better than "a chronically sick person infected with new diseases."[10]

Responding to these "cultural extremes," wrote Lu Xun, there emerged in Europe a "New Idealist School [新神思宗]" which included such figures as Stirner, Schopenhauer, Kierkegaard, and Ibsen, and Nietzsche—its most prominent representative. Lu Xun regarded Nietzsche as "the ultimate champion of individualism" who fought democracy's "leveling effects" and modern man's obsession with things material. In Lu Xun's opinion, Nietzsche and his "New Idealist School" represented "the new spirit of the twentieth century" that would "hew a way out" for mankind with their "will power."[11]

Influenced by Nietzsche and the "New Idealist School," Lu Xun's vision of a future China was quite different from that of most his contemporaries. While others dreamt of a modern state based on a certain degree of political democracy and buttressed by a powerful economy, Lu Xun envisioned China "turning from a country of loose sands [沙聚之國] into a country of men [人國]." The "country of men" was not a modern state but a community of noble individuals. The priority of China, therefore, was to "elevate man" [立人] by "promoting his individuality and ennobling his character."[12] Obviously neither entrepreneurs nor politicians were of much relevance in Lu Xun's plan. It was up to what Lu Xun called the "Satanic poets" to build a "country of men."*

---

* The word "Satanic poet" was first applied to Byron by his critics. Although Lu Xun borrowed the word from the history of English literature, he used "Mára poets" to

The concept of the "Satanic poets" is closely related to a theory about the "voice of heart" that Lu Xun proposed in his essay "On the Power of Satanic Poets" (March 1908):

> The most powerful thing a culture could leave to posterity is the voice of heart [心 聲]. Ancient people intuitively penetrated the mystery of nature, miraculously became one with the universe, and, communing with nature, they spontaneously expressed themselves and produced poems and songs.

These poems and songs constituted the "voice of heart" which was passed on from generation to generation, sustaining and invigorating a people. When a people could no longer access the "voice of heart" and fell silent, they would soon perish as a nation.[13]

As if to inform his readers of the theory's origin, Lu Xun wrote that "Nietzsche was surely correct when he attributed a rejuvenating power to primitive peoples."[14] Here Lu Xun was obviously referring to Nietzsche's theory of Greek tragedy and the "voice of heart" seems to derive from the Dionysian. In Lu Xun's view, the "voice of heart" had been missing in China's literary and philosophical traditions since ancient times. As a result the Chinese have always tried to avoid conflicts and seek peace, an attitude that will prove fatal to them, for "those who are reluctant to fight will bring upon themselves more wars than those who are willing to fight, and those afraid of death are more likely to perish than those who take their lives lightly."[15] The Chinese, however, need not despair. They should heed Nietzsche's message, which Lu Xun quoted from *Thus Spoke Zarathustra*:

> Once ancient sources are exhausted we will look for fountains of the future and for new origins. Oh my brothers, it will not be long before new lives originate and new fountains surge from the depth."[16]

Nietzsche seems to say that if the Chinese could not draw on their own pacifist tradition, they could still gain access to the "voice of heart" by turning to "new origins" or "new fountains."

What Lu Xun had in mind were "Satanic poets," that, as defined by Lu Xun, include "all those who are determined to resist and to take action, thereby incurring hostility from the public." Instead of "playing peaceful tunes to please the world," the Satanic poets "stir up people to contend with fate and to defy the world." Through their poems and their direct

---

translate the word "Satanic poets." Mára, a word from Sanskrit, refers to the "Devil" in Hindu legends.

involvement in revolutionary activities, these Satanic poets have infused a new life in their countrymen and, thereby, secured a respectable position for their country in the world. Among the "Satanic poets" discussed in Lu Xun's essay are Shelley, Pushkin, Lermontov, Mickiewicz, Slowacki, Krasinski and Petöfi as well as Byron, the archetype of "Satanic poets." Lu Xun thought it regrettable that these European Satanic poets were unknown to the Chinese and he raised a rhetorical question: "Where in China can one find warriors in the spiritual arena?"[17]

"Satanic poets" were characterized by Lu Xun as individuals who were able to fully realize their potentials due to their willingness to plunge into eternal conflicts.[18] The concept seems to derive from Nietzsche's tragic hero. But it is also related to a Nietzschean amoral will to power. Lu Xun found parallels between Satan in Byron's poem "Heaven and Earth" and Nietzsche's genealogy of morals:

> [In Byron's poem "Heaven and Earth" Satan says:] He [God] has defeated me and called me the evil one. If I had won, God would have been the evil one. Such a view of good and evil is different from that of Nietzsche. According to Nietzsche, the weak considers the strong to be evil because the latter has triumphed over him. Here "evil" stands for "strength." Nietzsche glorifies the strong in order to empower himself, Satan challenges the strong also in order to empower himself. Their views on good and evil may be different, their thirst for power, nonetheless, is the same.[19]

So far as the intention of Nietzsche's *Genealogy of Morals* is concerned, Lu Xun's comparison is quite beside the mark. There is, however, a kinship between Byron's Satan and Nietzsche's amoral will to power.

Nietzsche not only inspired Lu Xun to formulate new literary theories, he also gave Lu Xun a role model in the fictional figure Zarathustra. In the essay "On the Power of Satanic Poets," Lu Xun quoted Zarathustra as saying:

> I [Zarathustra] have gone so far ahead that I am all alone and without company. Turning back and looking at the civilized country and motley society: what a faithless society, what an unimaginative multitude! How can I stay in such a country? I am exiled from my own country. All I can hope for are the future generations.[20]

These words are an inaccurate translation from *Thus Spoke Zarathustra*. Nietzsche's philosophical intent was completely lost in the translation but the pathos of an alienated prophet was kept intact. Lu Xun must have seen Zarathustra af mirror of himself. Since going to Japan he had found most Chinese students and political activists there superficial and had kept a distance from them. He was at odds with his contemporaries on many issues. He must have felt vindicated and encouraged by the image of Zarathustra.

"On the Power of Satanic Poets" is an essay with a strong anti-social Darwinist tone. In contrast to some other Chinese reformers who looked up to Western powers and Japan as China's models, Lu Xun identified himself with the Indians, the Poles, the Jews, and other oppressed peoples. But the essay also shows Yan Fu's influence when its author accepted international conflicts as a welcome and necessary condition for progress. By the time he wrote his "Rebuttal of Devious Talks" (December 1908) he had broken with social Darwinism, in rhetoric as well as in spirit. In the essay he announced that a nation's worth did not lie in its military prowess or material wealth but in its people's noble character and artistic creativity. He believed that those Chinese who idolized imperialist powers must either have lost their mind because of their snobbishness or have accepted a slave identity due to prolonged subjection. He called those Chinese who advocated military expansion "beastly patriots."[21]

Lu Xun formulated a unique theory of evolution, one that was different from social Darwinism. He wrote:

> There are great differences between individuals in the process of human evolution: some remain at the stage of worms, others at the stage of apes. Such differences will not vanish for eons to come. Even if all men were able to reach a level of evolution simultaneously, the social order would have been disrupted the moment a single less advanced individual had appeared. For this single individual would be able to kill off all other peace-loving people, just like a wolf preying upon a flock of sheep.... On the one hand, men must not aggrandize their nation by invading and killing if they ever want to go beyond the stage of beasts.... On the other hand,... since war is unlikely to disappear and peace unlikely to last forever... it is necessary to defend oneself.[22]

Here evolution was defined as man's capacity for peace instead of for war. Lu Xun did not envision a utopia of ultimate peace, such as Kang Youwei's world of "Great Oneness," but an ethical world order whose relative peace has to be constantly guarded against violation. In the same essay Lu Xun praised Tolstoi for his noble ideal, but rejected his pacifism. In Lu Xun's view, the evolutionarily advanced—the "peace-loving people" had to fight back in order to survive the wars forced upon them by the evolutionarily retarded. The struggle was not about the "survival of the fittest" but the survival of a moral order. Thus Lu Xun, just as Liang Qichao before him, was able to turn the tables on social Darwinism.

Lu Xun's theory of man's ethical evolution was inspired by Nietzsche more than anyone else. The very metaphor about some men remaining at the stages of "worms" and "apes" came from Zarathustra's speech in the market place, "You have made your way from worm to man, and much in you is still worm. Once you were apes, and even now, too, man is more ape than any ape."[23] Lu Xun did not mistake Nietzsche for a Darwinist. In his "Rebuttal of Devious Talks," he associated Darwin with science and Nietzsche with faith:

> Selectively borrowing from the Darwinian theory of evolution, Nietzsche attacks Christianity and propounds the theory of superman. Although his theory is allegedly based on science, it smacks of religion and imagination. Obviously Nietzsche has no intention to abolish faith, he merely wants to replace the old faith with a new one... [Nietzsche's theory] has not become widely accepted yet: for unless one has an extraordinary command of science, one cannot expect to convince his audience by propagating his ideas under the guise of science. At any rate, his followers are all geniuses who are broad-minded, thorough in thinking, courageous, faithful, and defiant of public opinion.[24]

Having received no philosophical training at all, Lu Xun recognized neither the great chasm between his own theory and Nietzsche's new "faith" nor the need to define himself when using a phrase such as the "theory of evolution." In his later years, he talked about his early "bias of believing only in the theory of evolution,"[25] a vague statement that has misled scholars to assume a major influence from Darwin over the early Lu Xun.

Lu Xun also translated and published half a dozen short stories by eastern European authors during his stay in Japan, obviously an attempt to acquaint the Chinese with "Satanic poets" from Europe. Both his translations and his essays, though merely a young writer's first literary experiments, were of the finest quality by the standard of the time. But they were largely ignored by the reading public. Lu Xun had gone too far ahead of his time. The emerging consumers of Western literature in China were still captivated by melodramatic adaptations of Western novels. The literary works Lu Xun painstakingly selected and translated were too serious and difficult for them. So far as politically conscious intellectuals were concerned, be they revolutionaries or gradualists, Lu Xun's criticism of the modern West and his agenda to revive China through "Satanic poets" must have sounded completely irrelevant, if not also outrageous.

Lu Xun was disappointed at the public's response to his writings. He felt as if he were shouting among strangers who, neither agreeing with him nor raising objections, simply remained indifferent. He imaged himself standing alone in a boundless wasteland, completely at a loss. For quite a few years following his literary experiments he felt a "loneliness growing larger by the day," coiling around his soul "like a giant and deadly serpent." He suspected that he did not have a Satanic poet's charisma to rouse his countrymen to action.[26]

Lu Xun returned to China in 1909. The decision to leave Japan may have little to do with his disillusionment with his literary adventures. As eldest son of his family, Lu Xun felt obliged to help his widowed mother and his younger brother financially. He first taught classes and served as administrator in a school in his home province and since 1912 he served in the Ministry of Education of the newly founded republic in Nanjing and Beijing.* For nine years after his return to China, Lu Xun abandoned the stance of a "warrior in the spiritual arena" who was to enlighten the nation. As school teacher, school administrator and government bureaucrat, Lu Xun had to deal with particular individuals and situations on a daily basis. In the long run, such experiences must have contributed to a better understanding of men and society, an invaluable asset for a writer. In the short run, however, they seem to have made him more pessimistic about people's mentality and dampened his literary aspiration.

During the nine years, Lu Xun had almost completely cut himself off from literature. The only short story he wrote was "Reminiscence of the Past," an allegorical story about the 1911 Revolution, in which he described how members of China's social elite were panicked by an approaching revolution and how they continued their cowardly and depraved existence as the revolution proved to be merely a rumor. This short story would not have survived if the manuscript had not been rescued and published by his brother. For Lu Xun, dissatisfied with his creation, had submitted it to a wastebasket.[27]

When Lu Xun had, in his own words, "lost his youthful ardor," an era of youthful ardor dawned upon China—the era of the New Culture Movement. As if acting on Lu Xun's earlier exhortation, Chen Duxiu and other leading intellectuals took it upon themselves to bring about radical changes in people's mentality. These intellectuals seemed to fit into the profile of "Satanic poets" or "warriors in the spiritual arena." Ironically, Lu Xun, the prophet of the New Culture Movement, was in such a pessimistic mood that

---

* The Republic of China was founded in 1912 in Nanjing, Jiangsu. Soon in the same year the government moved to Beijing.

he was reluctant to join them. One day in the spring of 1918, Qian Xiantong, editor of *New Youth*, visited Lu Xun and asked him to write for the journal. Lu Xun replied:

> Suppose there were an iron room with no windows or doors, a room that would be virtually impossible to break out of. And suppose you had some people inside that room who were sound asleep. Before long they would all suffocate. In other words, they would slip peacefully from a deep slumber into oblivion, spared the anguish of being conscious of their impending doom. Now let's say that *you* came along and stirred up a big racket that awakened some of the lighter sleepers. In that case, they would go to a certain death, fully conscious of what was going to happen to them. Would you say that you had done those people a favor?[28]

Refusing to give up, the editor responded, "But since I've awakened at least *some* of them, you can't say that there is absolutely no hope for them to find a way out." The upshot of this conversation was Lu Xun's short story "The Diary of a Madman," followed by other short stories and many essays. This time the response was overwhelming. Almost overnight Lu Xun had established himself as the foremost short story writer and essayist in China. His very success as a writer after nine years of silence proved his grim view of China groundless: this was a society far more dynamic than he had imagined it to be.

Lu Xun carried his early admiration for Nietzsche over into the new era. Beside making references to him and quoting him, Lu Xun began to translate Nietzsche. By 1919 Nietzsche had already become a popular name in China. Yet none of his writings had been translated into Chinese, except a few sentences and paragraphs scattered here and there. Chinese readers must have been immensely gratified when the "Prologue" of *Thus Spoke Zarathustra*, translated by Lu Xun, appeared in *New Tide* in 1919. Though not a complete work, it was the next best thing they could expect.*

In the postscript to the translation, Lu Xun acknowledged that he had found *Thus Spoke Zarathustra* difficult to understand. His reason was "Nietzsche wrote too well and aphorisms in the book often appear self-contradictory."[29] The postscript is mainly a synopsis of the "Prologue" of

---

* The translation published in the journal *New Tide* was in vernacular Chinese. Lu Xun had previously translated the prologue into classical Chinese, a version that has never been published though its manuscript has survived and is now kept in the Lu Xun Museum in Beijing.

Thus Spoke Zarathustra, but it also contains a few explanatory comments that show how Lu Xun read and understood Nietzsche. About section six Lu Xun wrote:

> The tightrope walker refers to all heroes of bygone times, who made a living by taking risks. The masses may gather around to watch him, but they will disperse the moment he falls... The jester can have two meanings: he could be a utopian philosopher who caused the fall of the tight rope walker; or he could be Nietzsche himself: Nietzsche was also an idealist (according to G. Naumann). [This latter interpretation] may be incorrect (according to O. Gramzow).[30]

Lu Xun believed the gravediggers in section eight to be "mediocre historians who only gather things from the past and do not have an eye for the future." About the images of the eagle and the serpent in the tenth section, Lu Xun commented:

> The eagle and the serpent are both symbols: the serpent symbolizes wisdom and eternal recurrence and the eagle, pride and superman. The superman arises out of wisdom and pride; the masses are made of foolishness and pride. Foolishness and pride are the result of education.[31]

These comments reveal Lu Xun's lack of basic philosophical training but at the same time testify to the assiduous attention he paid to Nietzsche's words and images. However tangentially Lu Xun may have understood these words and images, he embraced what he thought he had learned from Nietzsche heart and soul.

Lu Xun attributed the success of his short stories to readers' ignorance of European continental literature. He particularly acknowledged his indebtedness to Gogol, Andreyev and Nietzsche:

> Around 1834, Gogol from Russia had already written "The Diary of a Madman" [The first story Lu Xun wrote for the *New Youth* bore the same title.]; around 1883, Nietzsche had already spoken through Zarathustra, 'You have made your way from worm to man, and much in you is still worm. Once you were apes, and even now, too, men are more ape-ish than any ape.' And the conclusion of "Drug" [one of Lu Xun's early short stories] apparently revealed a grisly Andreyevesque coldness. Nevertheless, in exposing the vices of the patriarchal system and the Confucian notion of propriety, the second version of "The Diary of a Madman" [referred to the short story by Lu Xun] expressed an anguish deeper and broader than Gogol's story, and it was less elusive than Nietzsche's superman.[32]

Two points were made about Nietzsche: Nietzsche had lent him the idea of man's ethical evolution and Nietzsche's concept of "superman" was an "elusive" one for him.

"The Diary of a Madman" (May 1918) was written in the first person. The hero is a paranoic obsessed with the idea that he lives in a cannibalistic society where "people are watching each other with deep suspicion, prepared to prey upon others and fearful of being preyed upon at the same time." The hero does not want to be part of this "banquet of human flesh" and is therefore persecuted by his family members and neighbors.

Through the mouth of the "madman," Lu Xun reformulated his earlier thoughts about man's ethical evolution,

> Way back in the beginning, it was probably the case that primitive peoples all ate some human flesh. But later on, because their ways of thinking changed, some gave up the practice and tried hard to improve themselves; they kept on changing until they became human beings, *true* human beings. But others didn't; they just kept right on with their cannibalism and stayed at that primitive stage.

These were the same ideas he had discussed in "Rebuttal of Devious Talks" ten years ago.*

Toward the end of the story, the madman, apparently imitating Zarathustra, exhorted his audience with the message of "*true* human beings,",

> You should change now! Change from the bottom of your hearts! You ought to know that in the future they're not going to allow cannibals in the world anymore. If you don't change, you're going to devour each other anyway. And even if a lot of you *are* left, a true human being is going to come along and eradicate the lot of you, just like a hunter getting rid of wolves—or reptiles![33]

Here Nietzsche's influence on Lu Xun was quite transparent. Lu Xun had modified the image of Zarathustra into that of a solitary hero, misunderstood and persecuted, but still trying to enlighten the others. Since Lu Xun considered the concept of superman to be "elusive," his "madman" did not talk about superman but called on people to be "*true* human beings."

"The Diary of a Madman" developed some key ideas Lu Xun had expressed in his Tokyo years. There was, however, one significant change. Lu Xun had shifted his attention from international relations to social and class relations within the Chinese society. Having applauded Nietzsche's critique of Western modernity ten years earlier, he now enlisted Nietzsche in his assault on China's tradition.

---

* See page 52.

One can hardly imagine an accusation of any society harsher than characterizing it as cannibalistic. Lu Xun gave his rationale when he employed the same metaphor on a different occasion:

> The so-called Chinese civilization is nothing but a banquet serving human flesh to the rich. The so-called China is nothing but a kitchen that hosts such a banquet.... Because of the many differences among people that are inherited from ancient times and continue to exist today, people are separated from each other, unable to feel each others' pain and suffering. Also, because each has a chance to enslave and eat others, he then forgets that one day he may also be enslaved and eaten. Thus, from the beginning of civilization to the present, numerous human flesh banquets, large and small, have been prepared. People are eating and being eaten in these banquets where the tragic wailing of the weak, not to mention women and children, is drowned in the joyous uproars of the stupid and murderous scoundrels.[34]

If Lu Xun had conceived the idea of ethical evolution when reading *Thus Spoke Zarathustra*, his social outlook was very different from that of Nietzsche. Lu Xun was a socialist by nature. His "*true* human beings" could well have been used as a footnote to young Karl Marx's "species beings." His condemnation of social hierarchy and social oppression could well have been written by a socialist from any other nation. But Lu Xun had not learned socialist theory yet. He believed that certain European nations, known to him through their best writers, were more advanced in ethical evolution and "cannibalism" was a rare case of primitivism existing only in China.

Lu Xun's comments on the Russian novelist Mikhail Artysbashev offer us more clues to his understanding of Nietzsche. Lu Xun considered Artysbashev's *Sanin*, the book that earned its author both popularity and notoriety, "decadent" and did not attach much importance to it. He translated three minor works by Artysbashev—two short stories "Luck," "The Doctor" and a short novel *Worker Shevoriv*, and gave them very sympathetic reviews.[35]

"Luck" tells the story of a prostitute who "entertained others with her body when she was pretty and continued to offer her [deformed] body for cruel entertainment after her nose had rotted away." It also tells how a sadistic servant abused the prostitute and was abused by others in turn. Its main theme, Lu Xun quoted Artysbashev, was that "not only the lucky squandered their lives, the unlucky also wasted theirs." The translated story, Lu Xun wrote, was meant as a mirror in which "all those who are over-satiated or who have starved" would shudder at their own images" when they realized that "they had also sought such entertainment or had entertained others." In Lu Xun's eyes, "Luck" must be a Russian author's indictment of cannibalistic society.[36]

"The Doctor" is a story about a doctor who refused to attend a dying police chief who had been wounded while leading a pogrom in a village. Lu Xun lauded the doctor as "a champion of justice for weak people," who formed a sharp contrast to what he conceived as typical Chinese mentality—indifference to the suffering of others. Lu Xun characterized the story as Artysbashev's "passionate resistance to the inhuman behavior of his compatriots." He wrote,

> It [the story] illustrates the entwinement of love and hate, and the resistance to the teaching of non-resistance. The writer is against non-resistance, since human beings by their nature cannot be without hate, a hate rooted in a broader love. Thus, Artysbasev is after all a disciple of Tolstoi, and at the same time a rebel against Tolstoi, to be more exact, he is a modifier of Tolstoism.[37]

Many years ago in Japan, in his essay "Rebuttal of Devious Talks," Lu Xun had expressed the idea that peace-loving peoples had to prepare to defend themselves against aggressors—the ethically retarded people.* Now he saw in "The Doctor" the same principle applied to social relations within a society. Obviously the doctor exemplified a "*true* human being" in Lu Xun's eyes.

Lu Xun discussed Artysbashev's short novel *Worker Shevoriov* in an essay he wrote shortly after he translated the work. Shevoriov was one of the reformers who had risked their lives for the "unlucky." After all his comrades had perished in struggles, Shevoriov alone lingered on as a fugitive. No one understood him, not to mention the "lucky," even the "unlucky" helped his pursuers hunt him down. In desperation, Shevoriov "was forced to resist the idea of non-resistance, and declared war on the unlucky as well as the lucky." The result was Shevoriov's "revenge on society."[38] (Towards the end of the story, armed with a handgun, Shevoriov went to a theatre and shot randomly into the crowd.) *Worker Shevoriov* seems to have combined the themes of both "Luck" and "The Doctor."

In the same essay Lu Xun argued that, despite Artysbashev's denial of his indebtedness to Nietzsche, the fictional figure worker Shevoriov represented Artysbashev's own ideal, and he "definitely reveals character traits of a Nietzschean man of strength, who, with all his power and will,

---

* See p. 52.

has fought a war until his death and who, with bombs and handguns, has resisted and fallen."[39] Lu Xun appended the German word "Untergehen" in parentheses after the word "fallen," apparently to show the idea's Nietzschean origin. [The Chinese word used to translate "Untergehen" is 沦灭.]

Lu Xun treated Nietzsche in a non-philosophical way. No conceptual rigor was attempted. Artysbashev, the anonymous observer in "Luck," the doctor, "a modified Tolstoi," and worker Shevoriov, all merged into a "Nietzschean man of strength." This was a man who rebelled against "the lucky" who abused others and, at the same time, despised "the unlucky" masses who, in addition to abusing themselves, joined "the lucky" in abusing others. The strength of the "Nietzschean man of strength" lay in his courage to sustain such a two front war and in his willingness to accept the fate of "falling (Untergehen)."

A "Nietzschean man of strength" was a new variation of "Satanic poets" or "warriors in the spiritual arena." It was also Lu Xun's ideal at this stage of his literary career. The role Lu Xun assigned to himself was, of course, not that of a bomb-throwing revolutionary like Shevoriov but that of a writer like Artysbashev.

In his short stories and essays Lu Xun depicted and analyzed people from all walks of life, peasants, domestic servants, and other lower class figures as well as politicians, literati and other persons from the ruling classes. His tone varied from work to work, ranging from satirical or sarcastic to naturalistic, from that of passionate appealing to that of reserved observation. Unveiling realities was his passion: he forced his readers to confront their own ignorance, insensitivity, selfishness, sadistic and masochistic tendencies, and hypocrisy. This was his strategy to mold the Chinese people into *true* human beings."

What Lu Xun called the "Nietzschean men of strength" have little resemblance to Nietzsche the philosopher. For Lu Xun *Thus Spoke Zarathustra* was first of all a literary work, a characterization of Zarathustra. When he referred to Artysbashev as a "Nietzschean of man of strength," he was merely expressing his opinion that the personality of the worker Shevoriov, Artysbashev's fictional figure, bore similarities to Zarathustra, Nietzsche's fictional figure.

Beside supplying Lu Xun with a powerful character with whom he could identify himself, *Thus Spoke Zarathustra* also served him as a collection of insightful observations and a treasure of rhetorical inventions. In his own writings, Lu Xun often consciously or unconsciously borrowed from the book. For example, in "Warrior and Flies," Lu Xun wrote,

> When a warrior has fallen in battle, the first thing flies notice is his blemishes and wounds. They suck them, humming, very pleased to think that they are greater heroes than the fallen warrior.... Yet the warrior for all his blemishes is a warrior, while the most whole and perfect flies are only flies.[40]

This may well have been inspired by "On the Flies of the Market Place" from *Thus Spoke Zarathustra*, in which Nietzsche called petty men "poisonous flies" and analyzed their behavior and psychology in comparison to noble-minded men. Not only the image of flies was borrowed, but the very essay was the development of one idea Nietzsche expressed there, "they ["poisonous flies"] think a lot about you [noble-minded men] with their petty souls—you always seem problematic to them. Everything that one thinks about a lot becomes problematic."[41]

Similar borrowings can be found in Lu Xun's prose poems "The Beggar," "Farewell of the Shadow," and "Wanderer." These poems were obviously inspired by "The Voluntary Beggar," "The Shadow" and "The Wanderer" from *Thus Spoke Zarathustra*. In these cases, Lu Xun had borrowed rhetorical devices rather than ideas from Nietzsche. The same is true when Lu Xun wrote that "Lies written in ink could never cover up facts written in blood. Debt in blood must be repaid in kind."[42] One does not find such a figure of speech in China's own literary past. It was an echo of Zarathustra's words: "Of all that is written I love only what a man has written with his blood. Write with blood, and you will experience that blood in spirit."[43] The intentions, however, were different: while Nietzsche was talking about the power of words, Lu Xun was referring to a tragic incident where students were killed in a government crackdown.

Of all the prominent writers of the New Culture Movement who had turned to Bolshevism, Lu Xun was one of the last. Having been concerned with a moral revival, Lu Xun watched with dismay as China was drifting into an era of mass politics galvanized by anti-imperialist sentiments. While many others applauded the May Fourth protests in 1919 as the awakening of the Chinese people, Lu Xun suspected it to be "an old-style awakening."[44] Having had no illusions about Western powers since his early years in Japan, he did not share the disillusionment of other intellectuals over the policy of the Western powers at the Paris Peace Conference. Lu Xun was glad to see several eastern European nations acquiring independence as a result of the conference. He contended that the most important issue for both the West and China should be that of ethical evolution. He warned that "doomed are those races that only blame others without self-reflection."[45] Lu Xun refused to change his role as a warrior in the spiritual arena.

Lu Xun felt deserted when his comrades-in-arms, one after another, turned to political radicalism or pure scholarship. In 1925 the killing of Chinese demonstrators by British police in Shanghai touched off a new wave of protests. Lu Xun found the Chinese reaction naive. Responding to a Chinese newspaper editorial that referred to the massacre as the "bankruptcy of a fake civilization," he wrote that "the civilization has been like this all the time…. A civilization that combines justice and military power has not appeared in the world yet." Again he warned his readers not to forget self-examination,

> When the British police brutally murder Shanghai residents, we are indignant and call out: the hypocritical civilized men have shown their true faces! … But has there been much protest when the Chinese gun-owning class plundered, burned and butchered people? Is it that we appreciate butchers "Made in China" when they brutalize people? Or is it that we are so barbaric that we are not surprised if a few Chinese are killed by other Chinese?[46]

The moral revival of the Chinese, Lu Xun believed, was more important than anti-imperialist agitation. In public speeches of the time, student activists often addressed their audience as "compatriots." Lu Xun advised them to contact people from all walks of life and form a realistic view of their "compatriots":

> Even if what you [the students] have discovered are not so much 'compatriots,' you can create [true compatriots] from scratch; even if what you have discovered is complete darkness, you can fight against the darkness."[47]

This was Lu Xun's invitation. He wanted to drag them from the political battlefield to the spiritual arena.

Closely associated with his concern for ethical evolution was Lu Xun's fundamental suspicion of politics. The mid-1920s was a dramatic period in China's socio-political history. There were two governments representing three main political forces at the time. One government was in Beijing, the capital of the Republic of China since 1912, dominated by military leaders who shared a conservative outlook. The other government was in Canton, a revolutionary government sustained by a united front of the Nationalists and the Communists since 1923. Although Lu Xun had served in various administrative positions in the Ministry of Education in the Beijing government, his relations with the ministry's conservative chiefs were often strained, to say the least.* Neither was he interested in the revolutionary government in the south. As late as 1925, in a letter he confided to Xu Guangping, one of his students, his future wife:

> There are two kinds of "-ists" active in China. Both appear to be brand new but, I believe, they are still the old stuff. At this moment I belong to neither party, though I hope they will recognize their mistakes and change for the better.[48]

From the same letter we know that the first of the "two kinds of '-ists'" refers to "internationalists," meaning the Communists and the Nationalists who joined hands in a revolutionary movement under the auspices of the Comintern and the second refers to anarchists. In Lu Xun's view, these political activists failed to address the key issue: people's mentality. He put it bluntly, "it will come to no good end if slaves are entrusted to manage a house." Without abandoning the mentality of slaves, "no matter what system is created, autocracy or republic, or any other systems, it is no more than selling the same old merchandise under a new logo."[49]

By the mid-1920s, few of the leading intellectuals in China still shared Lu Xun's distrust of politics. Lu Xun experienced a crisis which he recorded in frank and vivid terms in a series of short prose poems he wrote during 1924 and 1925. He also confided to Xu Guangping that he "often feels that only 'darkness and nothingness' are 'reality.'" Nevertheless he would rather agree with Petöfi's poetic statement, "desperation is just as absurd as hope," and he was to put up a "desperate resistance." Lu Xun perceived his own task as "preparing warriors for the 'thought revolution.'" The decisive battle would be fought in the future when the "warriors are well trained." Therefore his activities, echoing Zarathustra's words, "have nothing to do with the present society." Never a utopian, Lu Xun did not imagine that his effort would bring about changes overnight. What he hoped for was a future "a little bit better" than the present.[50]

Lu Xun's experiences in 1926 and 1927 forced him to reexamine his views. In March 18, 1926, in front of a government building, soldiers opened fire on student demonstrators, killing forty-seven students, including several from the Teachers College for Women, whom Lu Xun had taught. Lu Xun was infuriated at the event and he wrote essays to express his grief and indignation. He anguished over the fact that he could offer no more help than "empty words."[51] Lu Xun remembered the event's impact on him,

---

* Lu Xun held teaching positions in several colleges in Beijing since 1921. For his moral support of progressive students, he was even expelled from the ministry for a period.

> It was when students were killed by gunshots [on March 18, 1926.] and censorship was tightened that I had the following thought: literature is the profession of the most useless and powerless people. Those who have power do not open their mouth: they kill. When the oppressed begin to speak and write, they are killed. Even if they manage to survive and continue to cry out, to moan, and to protest, they can do nothing about those in power who continue to oppress, to mistreat, and to kill. In such circumstances what can literature do for them?[52]

Lu Xun began to view war and revolution in a new perspective. In July 1926 Lu Xun made the following comments on Boris Pilnyak's *Ivan and Marya*,

> As a witness and participant in the revolution, he [Pilnyak] realized that revolution [the Russian Bolshevik Revolution], for all its destruction, bloodshedding, and chaos, is not without creativity. Therefore he is completely free from despair. This is how a man who is truly alive feels in the era of revolution.... While many artists and writers have wilted during the season of revolution, many others plunged themselves into the mountain-shattering and earth-breaking new waves, either devoured by it or wounded in it. The devoured have perished; the wounded continue to live and explore a new life, humming their tunes of suffering and joy. When they have passed away, a new age will emerge and a new kind of art and literature will be created.[53]

Such exuberant praise of the Russian Bolshevik Revolution did not signal Lu Xun's turn to Bolshevism. Pilnyak was not a Bolshevik. His position is well described by Robert Payne,

> For Pilnyak the Russian revolution was never anything so simple as a war between the Bolsheviks and the rest. He saw it as a sudden release of primitive energy; vast ancestral forces were at work; and all Russian history, and all the ancient customs of the Russian people, were implicated.... Old traditions had broken beneath the weight of history, and what was left was a surging mass of desperate people searching for a new way of life, a new understanding.[54]

Whether Pilnyak was influenced by Nietzsche or not, his picture of the Russian Revolution has much in common with the kind of national revival Lu Xun had envisioned since his youth.* Pilnyak's story seems to have served as a catalyst for Lu Xun's acceptance of political revolution, especially at a moment when he painfully felt the futility of literature.

---

* According the Robert Payne, when twenty-one years old, Pilnyak, in his short story "Above the Ravine," wrote with sympathy about the life of an eagle from the eagle's viewpoint. One wonders if he, like Gorky who wrote "Song of the Falcon," had been exposed to Nietzsche's influence.

Lu Xun made the aforementioned comments on Pilnyak's novel shortly after the Canton government issued the order for the Northern Expedition. Lu Xun may have harbored a wish that "mountain-shattering, earth-breaking new waves" of war and revolution would erupt in China. For the moment, however, this was no more a fleeting fantasy. He had no intention to be part of any revolution. As a result of his denunciation of the killing of the students, he had run afoul of the authorities in Beijing. In August he left Beijing for Xiamen to assume a teaching position there. He decided to steer clear of politics and devote himself to teaching and writing for at least two years.

Xiamen proved to be a place where he could hardly continue the quiet life of a writer and scholar. He was embittered by the way he was treated by the university authorities and he felt himself surrounded mostly by people with "the skin of scholars and the bones of slaves." In the end of 1926, he accepted an invitation to teach in the School of Liberal Arts of Sun Yat-sen University in Canton. This brought him into the whirlpool of revolution.

Now Lu Xun began to identify his literary career with the ongoing national revolution jointly propelled by the Nationalists and the Communists. When invited to deliver a speech in the Whompoa Military Academy in April 8, 1927, Lu Xun revealed his new thought about the relation between literature and revolution. He believed that literature, in the beginning, was the protest of oppressed peoples. Once people realized the futility of mere protest, their "songs of distress" would turn into "angry uproars" and a "great revolution" would follow. In the era of "great revolution" people would be too busy to be concerned with literature. Lu Xun praised the cadets for their role in the revolutionary war. He admitted that he found "the sound of cannon far more charming than the sound of literature."[55]

Although excited at the victorious marching of the National Revolutionary Army, he was by no means without ambivalent feelings. Since coming to Canton, the base of the National Revolutionary Army, he had found the city, just like other cities, dominated by soldiers and merchants. People's mentality had not undergone the slightest change. Lu Xun was afraid of that the revolution would only appear victorious without shaking the foundation of the old society just as the 1911 Revolution.*[56]

---

* For his view on the 1911 Revolution, see p. 54

The event took an unexpected turn. In April 12, 1927 Chiang Kai-shek staged a coup and in the next few months the Nationalists rounded up and executed thousands of Communists and their sympathizers. Some of Lu Xun's friends and acquaintances were among the victims. The prospect of a "great revolution" had disappeared. Now a cannibalistic society had grown from a nightmarish metaphor into a reality. Lu Xun experienced, in his words, an "unprecedented terror." The self-doubt he had about his role as a writer had grown into the painful realization that his previous attacks on cannibalism were completely ineffective. After seeing young men being killed in the *coup* by their former comrades, also young men, Lu Xun abandoned his belief that a younger generation was always better than the old one and he came to the conclusion that something else must be done.[57]

Not until 1929-1930 had Lu Xun learned much about Marxism. But from what he had learned from Pilnyak and other "fellow travelers," he at least recognized in the Russian Bolshevik Revolution—his model of a "great revolution"—a class war waged by the oppressed against the oppressors. Since 1926 a new tendency can be discerned in Lu Xun's writings. He no longer treated the oppressed classes as accomplices and perpetrators of the cannibalistic society. He had become far more sympathetic toward them and begun to focus his firepower on the oppressing classes.

Around 1928 Lu Xun began a comprehensive study of Soviet literary theories and Soviet literature, mainly through Japanese translations. Between then and 1931 the total volume of Soviet literature and theoretical works he had translated into Chinese was far greater than that of his own writings.[58] Although never a member of the Chinese Communist party, Lu Xun, influenced by Soviet writers, had been converted to Bolshevism. Since then he no longer regarded himself as a warrior single-handedly fighting the dark forces of cannibalism but as part of the communist movement working for a world built on different principles.

Lu Xun's conversion was not an abrupt break with his past. It is not accidental that those Soviet writers that impressed Lu Xun most either had been under Nietzsche's influence or had expressed ideas that appeared to be Nietzschean. One of these was Maxim Gorky, a writer whose indebtedness to Nietzsche well recognized by his contemporaries and later researchers.[59] In the 1930s when Lu Xun had already joined the left-wing literary movement, he translated some of Gorky's early short stories, obviously drawn to their Nietzschean themes. Of all Soviet writers, as Lundberg put it, "the greatest influence on Lu Xun was certainly played by Lunacharsky."[60] Lunacharsky, himself once an admirer of Nietzsche, spoke a language that was understandable and appealing to Lu Xun. Lu Xun translated a short article by a Japanese scholar who made the following summary of Lunacharsky's ideas:

> The so-called civilization [the modern civilization] is a decadent one. It is certainly not a civilization hoped for by men who are truly alive. Although there may be certain types of beauty, elegance, or good taste in it, there is nothing one can call a will to resistance, as a result it has stagnated as if it were dead. We need efforts, tensions, and struggles and we are not afraid of the inherent tragedy and sacrifice. After all, people of our time will never be happy until a fruitful and powerful new civilization is founded.[61]

These views about the contemporary civilization, "resistance" and "a fruitful and powerful new civilization" were not strange to Lu Xun at all. Lu Xun himself had learned similar ideas from Nietzsche when he was in Japan. As we may expect, Lunacharsky struck him as "extremely insightful."[62]

Lu Xun had another reason to be grateful to Lunacharsky. For several years he had been constantly attacked as a reactionary by Guo Moruo and a few other self-proclaimed "proletarian writers." When he learned that Lunacharsky treated Leo Tolstoi, a non-Bolshevik writer, as a "fellow traveler," not an enemy, he considered the Russian Marxist critic to be a very "humane and tolerant" person. Lu Xun was willing to perceive himself as a "fellow traveler" who, according to a Soviet writer, might grow into a "proletarian writer" in the process of revolution.[63] Besides, Lunacharsky applauded Leo Tolstoi' criticism of the bourgeois society but rejected his teaching of non-resistance, a position shared by Lu Xun in his "Rebuttal of Devious Talks" and his comments on Artysbashev's "Doctor."*

Lu Xun was especially drawn to Lunacharsky's play *Don Quixote Liberated*. He had once begun to translate the play only to give it up after realizing that both the Japanese and German translations, on which he based his own, were abridged versions. When his friend, Qu Qiubai, translated the play from the Russian original, Lu Xun's joy was, in his own words, "beyond expression." Lu Xun wrote a "postscript" for the translated play, in which he quoted Lunacharsky's personification of two opposing social

---

* See p. 52 and p. 59.

ideals. On the one hand, there was Graf Murzio, the incarnation of autocracy, who spoke to Don Quixote about "the happiness of the beasts":

> Oh! Don Quixote, you don't understand our beasts. A wild beast bites a small deer's head, breaks its throat, slowly sucking its warm blood, feeling the trembling of the deer's legs underneath its claws and the gradually passing of its life—How sweet it is. But humans are delicate beasts. You rule and live a luxurious life, forcing others to pray for you, to bow to you out of fear, and to be humiliated before you. Happiness consists in feeling in your hand the power of making millions of people surrender to you unconditionally: they become like slaves and you like God... Breaking all laws of men and of God, creating laws according to your own will, and forming new chains for others. Power, this word covers all—this is a miraculous and intoxicating word. Life should be measured by the level of power. Whoever does not have power is but a corpse.

Apparently Lu Xun recognized in Graf Murzio a champion of cannibalistic society, who spoke a Nietzschean language.

On the other hand, there is Drigo Pazz, the incarnation of the principle of revolution, who, taught Don Quixote the necessity of a revolutionary dictatorship, also in a Nietzschean language:

> Yes, we are autocratic devils. We are dictators. Look at this sword—it kills with precision, just like the swords of the aristocrats. But their swords kill for the system of slavery, our swords kill for freedom.... During this short period we are oppressors... soon our oppression will make it impossible for anyone to oppress others in the world.

Lu Xun observed that Don Quixote, who had the good intention to fight for social justice, was doomed to fail due to his "wrong strategy" and he called Drigo a "warrior with correct strategy and an unwavering will." Apparently, Lu Xun saw in Don Quixote his old ideal of a "Nietzschean man of strength." Now he accepted the Bolshevik dictatorship as an effective means to end cannibalism.[64]

Lunacharsky's dramatization of moral and social struggles made it easier for Lu Xun to accept the Bolshevik revolution. He also helped Lu Xun regain a sense of mission as a writer. Here again Nietzsche's influence on both the Russian writer and the Chinese writer could be felt. For it is Nietzsche, as Bernice Rosenthal puts it, who "provided Lunacharsky with a means to reconcile aestheticism and Marxism, to argue that art can change consciousness, and is thus a powerful weapon in the revolutionary struggle."[65]

Now a warrior in the spiritual arena no longer needed to confront the dark forces single-handedly, he could be part of a revolution that, with the support of the masses, employing both pen and gun, would eventually smash the cannibalistic society. Lu Xun's conversion to Bolshevism brought a change to his writing. The pessimistic, albeit heroic, tone of his previous writings was gone, he began to write with unprecedented clarity and confidence.

Beside Lunacharsky's writing, Fadeyev's novel *The Rout* had a great impact on Lu Xun.* The story is set in the Russian Far East during the Civil War (1918-1920). It tells how a band of Red guerrilla fighters, after a bloody battle and many casualties, managed to break the siege of a combined force of Kolchak's troops and Japanese troops. Considering the fact that the Chinese Red Army, besieged by Chiang Kai-shek's troops, was fighting for its very survival, Lu Xun could not have missed the parallel when he translated the novel and recommended it to the Chinese readers.

Beyond its obvious political implication, *The Rout* also helped Lu Xun clarify his own thought and offered him a new ideal. Lu Xun was especially impressed by two characters in the novel. One was Metik, a guerrilla soldier who used to be a student. This Metik, according to Lu Xun, "felt himself full of ambition at one moment, and full of despair at another, eventually resigned himself... to savoring his own solitude." Lu Xun commented that Metik was not a true revolutionary and the brutal realities had made a mockery of reformers like Metik who "patiently waited for the appearance of god-like prophets and gentleman-like masses."[66] Obviously Lu Xun recognized in Metik his own weakness and flaws.

Levinson, the captain of the guerrilla group, was also an intellectual, but of a different type. In the postscript to his translation of *The Rout*, Lu Xun quoted extensively from the novel what had impressed him most. Levinson seems to share Lu Xun's concern over the seemingly unbridgeable chasm between the abysmal conditions of humanity and the ideal "*true* human beings":

> The ultimate meaning of his [Levinson's] existence lies in overcoming all these scarcities and difficulties. Had he had no such longing for a new, beautiful, strong and kind mankind, a powerful longing unmatched by any other longing, Levinson would have been a different person. But when millions of people are forced to spend their lives in such primitive and miserable conditions, in such

---

* Lu Xun wrote in 1930, "As far as I know, Lunacharsky's *Don Quixote Liberated*, Fadeyev's *The Rout*, and Gladkov's *Cement* are works that are incomparably better than anything produced in China in the past eleven years." *Complete Works*, vol. 4, 207.

senselessly poverty, how can one talk about a new and beautiful mankind?

Levinson, in Lu Xun's view, has the right answer: one should lead the suffering masses to fight for a "new, beautiful, strong and kind mankind."[67]

Lu Xun was particularly impressed by how the novel portrays the relations between Levinson and his soldiers. The masses, Levinson believes, have the instinct to sacrifice their lives for a noble goal, but this instinct is "buried" in their "minute, trivial needs and concerns, because everyone... is weak." Therefore the masses, "acknowledging their weakness," "leave their greatest concerns to stronger men" while carrying on their "ordinary, minute tasks." Levinson belongs to such "stronger men." He "cautiously makes plans for his troop, tries to hide his emotion, manages to win loyalty from the soldiers." Even so, tension exists between "stronger men" and the masses. In times of crisis, the soldiers "watch him [Levinson] with awe and fear, but without sympathy." Levinson even feels that he is "an alien force above his troops." To keep the soldiers in line, he has to "wield power" over them.[68]

The fictional Levinson provided a new ideal for Lu Xun. Levinson, one of the "stronger men," was not a negation, but rather the destiny of a "Nietzschean man of strength" in the era of revolution. Both ideals were fighting for a new mankind and both shared a sense of distance between themselves—the heroic and enlightened few and the mundane masses. "Nietzschean men of strength" would naturally turn into Bolshevik "stronger men" if only they ended their war with the masses and began to lead them. Lu Xun had not turned away from Nietzsche to Bolshevism, but from an old Nietzschean vision created by himself and Artysbashev to a new one created by Lunacharsky and Fadeyev.[69]

Before he discovered Bolshevik heroes through Soviet literature, Lu Xun had already found a "Nietzschean man of strength" questionable, as indicated by his remark on "Worker Shevoriov" in August 1926:

> Toward the end [of the novel *Worker Shevoriov*] Shevoriov's thought was extremely horrible. He began with working for the society. When the society persecuted him and even attempted to kill him, he suddenly turned against it to seek vengeance. All have turned into enemies and all are to be destroyed.[70]

Since 1926, Lu Xun made fewer references to Nietzsche and, when he did, the tone was often critical. For example, in his preface to a short story collection, Lu Xun called attention to Nietzsche's influence on several Chinese writers including himself and he remarked:

> Nietzsche taught people to prepare for the emergence of the "superman." If the

"superman" does not appear, the preparation would come to nothing. Nietzsche, however, had his way out: madness and death. Otherwise he would have to accept nothingness or resist it. Even if he did not seek petty happiness in his solitude as the "last man" did, all he could do was to defy authorities and degenerate into a nihilist.[71]

Given the sarcastic tone, his criticism was a measured one. After all, Nietzsche was well-intentioned, at least better than the "last man," and not yet a "nihilist." His only error was the lack of an effective program.

Although Zarathustra had now fallen short of an ideal hero, the book *Thus Spoke Zarathustra* continued to fascinate Lu Xun. It was during the 1930s that he encouraged and sponsored its first complete Chinese translation. In his writings he continued to adapt rhetoric devices and ideas from the book. Imitating, for example, "The Night Song" from *Thus Spoke Zarathustra*, a lyrical and philosophical prose poem, he wrote a "Night Song," a political prose poem about the "immense darkness" of China under the Nationalist government. He called scholars supporting the Nationalist government "preachers of death," and accused the ruling class of trying to turn young people into "der letzte Mensch" by denying them access to good foreign literature.[72] It is obvious that after turning to Bolshevism, he continued to perceive the world in the eyes of Zarathustra, a Zarathustra that had been reinvented by Soviet Bolshevik intellectuals and himself.

The time between 1929 and 1934 was a pleasant period for Lu Xun. During this period he cooperated well with the CCP in promoting China's left-wing literary movement and had developed friendship and mutual respect with some of the CCP's leading activists such as Qu Qiubai and Feng Xuefeng. After Qu Qiubai and Feng Xuefeng left Shanghai in 1933 and 1934 successively, Lu Xun's situation became difficult. Now the left-wing literary movement in Shanghai was directed by Zhou Yang and a few other CCP members in Shanghai who did not view Lu Xun as a friend and comrade. To the Zhou Yang group Lu Xun was just one of "fellow travelers" who was supposed to follow their orders. They could not tolerate the fact that a number of independent-minded writers seemed to have formed a circle around Lu Xun. In order to enforce conformity within the left-wing literary movement, the Zhou Yang group orchestrated anonymous attacks on Lu Xun's friends in newspapers and journals. They refrained from attacking Lu Xun directly due to his prestige, but tried to pressure him into abandoning his friendship with writers they deemed too independent. Lu Xun confided to a friend that he could not make his voice heard in the

League of Left-wing Writers and that he always felt that he was "bound in an iron chain while a foreman was whipping [him] on the back."*[73] Lu Xun was again forced to fight a two-front war, in his words, guarding his rear from "so-called comrades" while "fighting enemies in the front."

Toward the end of 1935 the relations between Lu Xun and the Zhou Yang group reached a breaking point. When the latter, following orders from the Comintern, began to advocate a popular front policy and disbanded the League of Left-wing Writers without even consulting Lu Xun, Lu Xun felt himself and the revolution betrayed. In three allegorical historical stories and a poem he wrote in December 1935, Lu Xun portrayed the Zhou Yang group as unprincipled, self-seeking opportunists and hinted that he might break with the movement controlled by the group.[74] It was an extremely difficult and painful decision to make. Working as part of the well organized and disciplined communist movement had been his *raison d'être* in the past seven years. Leaving this movement would have meant either returning to the futile position of a "Nietzschean man of strength" or completely abandoning his fight against cannibalism. Over the next few months, Lu Xun continued his two-front war—against both his enemies and his "friends."

The dilemma that had been tormenting him unexpectedly resolved itself. On April 25, 1936, his friend Feng Xuefeng, who had left Shanghai two years ago, suddenly turned up in his home. Feng Xuefeng had traveled a long way from Yanan, the Red Army's new base since late in 1935, with the mission to reestablish severed connection between the party's central leadership and its underground organization in Shanghai. Before leaving Yanan, Feng Xuefeng had a conversation with Mao Zedong, the CCP's Chairman, and was instructed to show special respect for Lu Xun.[75] Feng Xuefeng stayed in Lu Xun's home for two weeks and told Lu Xun many things about the Chinese Red Army, its battles against the encircling Nationalist troops, the Long March, the new base areas in northern China, and Mao Zedong's policy on a united front against the Japanese invasion. Considering how Lu Xun had been moved by the story of Fadeyev's fictional guerrilla band, it is quite understandable that he was now mesmerized by these real-life stories. His crisis was over. He could leave behind his unpleasant experiences with the Zhou Yang group and continue

---

* The League of Left-wing Writer was a front organization of the CCP. Lu Xun was one of its founding members and he had served in its Executive Committee).

to identify himself with the Communist movement embodied in the Red Army and Mao Zedong. Five days after Feng Xuefeng's arrival, Lu Xun wrote an essay, in which he made a strained reinterpretation of his historical story "Exit from the Pass," emphatically denying its pessimistic implications.[76]

With Feng Xuefeng's support, Lu Xun threw off all restraints and fought back when he and his friends were again attacked by the Zhou Yang group. The ensuing open debate between Lu Xun and the Zhou Yang group reflected a policy difference between Mao Zedong and the Comintern in regard to the United Front. The Zhou Yang group, following instructions from the Comintern, emphasized cooperation with other political forces. Lu Xun (and Feng Xuefeng) supported Mao Zedong's view that the CCP should maintain its revolutionary stand and play a leading role within the United Front.

Viewed in a broader context, the conflict between the Lu Xun circle and the Zhou Yang group goes beyond a mere case of "struggles between the two lines" within the communist movement. What angered Lu Xun so much was not merely the other side's view on a particular issue but also the unscrupulous manipulation used by the other side to enforce conformity. Lu Xun's fight can be seen as an individual's defense of his intellectual independence and moral integrity against organized coercion.[77]

In the last months of his life, lying sick in bed, Lu Xun seemed to be revisited by that proud and defiant Nietzsche he knew in Japan. His words about his imminent death echoed Zarathustra,

> According to Zhuang Zi, it does not matter where you leave a dead body, for it will perish just the same, "whether devoured by the birds up in the air or the ants down in the earth."
>
> I am not so generous, though. If my flesh and blood are to feed beasts, I prefer to feed lions, tigers and eagles. Not one scrap will I give to mangy curs.
>
> When lions, tigers, and eagles are well fed, they afford a magnificent spectacle in the sky, on cliffs, amid deserts and jungles. Even when captured and kept in a zoo, or killed and stuffed as specimens, they are still a fine sight which drives petty thoughts from the mind.
>
> But if you fatten a pack of mangy curs, all they can do is to rush madly about and whine—disgusting![78]

It was an uncanny premonition. Lu Xun died on Oct 29, 1936. Since then, his complex legacy, including the many facets of his appropriation of

Nietzsche, has been continuously claimed by very different people. Lu Xun lived on, and so did the Zarathustra that had become part of him since his youth.

Notes

[1] His original name was Zhou Shuren. Lu Xun was his pen name by which he has been known by most readers.

[2] Lu Xun, "Preface" to *Cheering from the Sidelines*, in *Complete Works of Lu Xun* [《鲁迅全集》] (Beijing: People's Literature Press, 1981), vol. 1, 415. The translation is based on *Diary of a Madman and Other Stories*, trans. by William A. Lyell (Honolulu: University of Hawaii Press, 1990), 24.

[3] Lu Xun, *Complete Works*, vol. 1, 416.

[4] "Lu Xun's letter to Jiang Yizhi," (Oct., 1904), *Ibid.*, vol. 11, 321–324.

[5] "Mr. Jujino," (Oct 12, 1926), *Complete Works*, vol. 2, 302-400.

[6] *Ibid.* and *Complete Works*, vol. 1, 415-416.

[7] Xu Shoushang, *The Lu Xun I Know* [《我所認識的鲁迅》] (Beijing: People's Literature, 1952), 8-9. The translation is that of Lennart Lundberg, see his *Lu Xun As a Translator: Lu Xun's Translation and Introduction of Literary Theory, 1903-1936* (Stockholm: Orientaliska Studier Stockholom University, 1989), 41.

[8] Some Japanese writers also influenced Lu Xun, see Ito Toramaru, *Lu Xun and the Japanese: the Modernity of Asia and the Concept of "Individuality"* [伊藤虎丸, 《鲁迅と日本人，アジアの近代と「個」の思想》] (Tokyo: Asahi Shinbon Press, 1983).

[9] "A Lesson of the History of Science," *Complete Works*, vol. 1, 25–43.

[10] "On Cultural Extremes," *Complete Works*, vol. 1, 46, 48, 50, 55-57.

[11] *Ibid.*, 55-56.

[12] *Ibid.*, 56-57.

[13] "On the Power of Satanic Poets," *Complete Works*, vol. 1, 63-64.

[14] *Ibid..*

[15] *Ibid.*, 69.

[16] *Ibid.*, 63. Lu Xun's translation was not literal. For the English translation, see Walter Kaufmann, *Portable Nietzsche* (New York: Penguin Books, 1976), 323.

[17] *Complete Works*, vol. 1, 66, 98-100.

[18] *Ibid.*, 66-68.

[19] *Ibid.*, 77-79.

[20] *Ibid.*, 49. The section he quoted is "On the Land of Education" from Part Two of *Thus Spoke Zarathustra*.

[21] *Complete Works*, vol. 8, 33-34.
[22] *Ibid.*, 31-32.
[23] *Portable Nietzsche*, 124.
[24] *Complete Works*, vol. 8, 28–29.
[25] See also Ito Toramaru's eloquent discussion of Lu Xun's theory of evolution, *Lu Xun and Eschatology* [伊藤虎丸,《魯迅と終末論》] (Tokyo: 龍溪書店, 1975), 184-203.
[26] Lu Xun, "Preface to *Cheering from Sideline*," *Complete Works*, vol. 1, 416–418. The translation is based on Lyell, 1990, 25.
[27] Lu Xun's "Reminiscence of the Past" is well discussed in William A. Lyell, Jr. *Lu Hsün's Vision of Reality* (Berkeley: University of California Press, 1976).
[28] *Complete Works*, vol. 1, 418–419. The translation is based on Lyell, 1990, 27.
[29] "The translator's postscript to *Zarathustra's Prologue*," *Complete Works*, vol. 10, 439-441.
[30] *Ibid.*
[31] *Ibid.*
[32] "Preface to the *China's New Literature: Short Stories Series 2*," [《中國新文學大系》小說二集序.] in *Complete Works*, vol. 6, 238-265.
[33] Lu Xun, *Diary of a Madman*, *Complete Work*, vo. 1, 422; the translation is based on Lyell, 1990: 38-40.
[34] "Random Scribbling Under the Lamp," (April 1925), *Complete Works*, vol.1, 210-219. The translation is based on Lyell, 1990, 345.
[35] Lu Xun, "After Translating *Worker Sheveriov*," "Translator's postscript to '*Luck*'," and "Translator's note to 'The *Doctor*'," *Complete Works*, vol. 10, 165-171, 172-174, and 176-177.
[36] *Complete Works*, vol. 10, 172-175.
[37] *Complete Works*, vol, 10, 176-177. Also see Lunburg, 1989, 79.
[38] "After Translating *Worker Shevoriov*," *Complete Works*, vol. 10, 165-171.
[39] *Ibid.*.
[40] "Fighters and Flies," *Complete Works*, vol. 3, 38–39. The translation is based on *Selected Works*, translated by Xianyi Yang and Gladys Yang (Beijing: Foreign Languages Press, 1956), vol. 2, 133.
[41] "On the Flies of Market Place," *Portable Nietzsche,* 163-164.
[42] Lu Xun, "More Roses without Blooms," *Selected Writings*, translated by Xianyi Yang and Gladys Yang, vol. 2, 260.
[43] *Portable Nietzsche*, 152.
[44] Lu Xun, "Preface of the Translator" (written on August 2, 1919) *Complete Works*, vol. 10, 192-193.

[45] Lu Xun, "Discontent," (published on Nov. 1, 1919) *Complete Works*, vol. 1, 358-359.
[46] Lu Xun, "Random Thoughts," *Complete Works*, vol. 3, 88–99.
[47] *Ibid.*.
[48] Lu Xun, "Letters to Xu Guangping," March 31, 1925, *Complete Works*, vol. 11, 30-34.
[49] *Ibid.*
[50] Lu Xun to Xu Guangping (March 18, 1925), *Complete Works*, vol. 11, 19-22; Lu Xun, "Correspondence," (March 12, 1925) *Complete Works*, vol. 3, 22; also see the poem "Hope" in *Wild Grass*.
[51] For examples see "Roses without Flowers, No.2," "Sphere of Death," "In Memory of Liu Hezheng," and "Empty words," in *Complete Works*, vol. 3, 261-283.
[52] Lu Xun, "The Literature in the Epoch of Revolution," (Lu Xun's speech to Whompoa cadets on April 8, 1927, *Complete Works*, vol. 3, 417.
[53] Lu Xun, "Diary on Horse, No. 2," *Complete Works*, vol. 3, 341–343.
[54] Robert Payne's introduction in Boris Pilnyak's *The Tale of the Unextinguished Moon and Other Stories*, translated by Beatrice Scott (New York: Washington Square Press, 1967), xii-xiii.
[55] Lu Xun, "The Literature in the Epoch of Revolution," (Lu Xun's speech to Whompoa cadets on April 8, 1927, *Complete Works*, vol. 3, 417-426.
[56] Lu Xun, "On the Bell Tower," *Complete Works*, vol. 4, 29-37; and "The Silent China," *Complete Works*, vol. 4, 11-15.
[57] For examle, in "A Repsonse to Mr. Youhen," *Complete Works*, vol. 3, 453-454 and "Preface to *Three Leisures Collection*," *Complete Works*, vol. 4, 5.
[58] For a thorough and insightful study of Lu Xun's translation and intruduction of Soviet literary theory and Soviet literature see Lennart Lundberg, *Lu Xun As a Translator: Lu Xun's Translation and Introduction of Literary Theory, 1903-1936* (Stockholm: Orientaliska Studier Stockholom University, 1989).
[59] See Rosenthal's "Introduction" in *Nietzsche in Russia*, 13-14 and Mary Louise Loe's "Gorky and Nietzsche: the Quest for a Russian Superman" in the same book, 251-273.
[60] Lundberg, 122-127, 134-135.
[61] Lunacharsky, *Literature and its Criticisms*, trans. by Lu Xun (Shanghai, Foam Press, Oct. 1929), 3-4.
[62] Lu Xun's "Preface" to his translation of Lunacharsky's *Foundation of Pragmatic Aesthetics*, and his "Translator's Postscript" to his translation of Lunacharsky's *Literature and its Criticism*, *Complete Works*, vol.10, 294-303. For his own views about the contemporary civilization in 1907 and 1908 when he was in Japan, see p. 49 and p. 51.
[63] About Lu Xun's response to Lunacharsky's criticism of Tolstoi, see *Complete Works*, vol. 10, 298-303; about the relation between fellow travelers and revolutionaries, see "Postscript" to the Chinese translation of A. Iakovlev's *October*, *Complete Works*, vol. 10, 320.

⁶⁴ Postscript to *Don Quixote Liberated*, 《被解放了的唐吉訶德》後記，《集外集拾遺》 *Complete Works*, vol. 7, 397-404.
⁶⁵ Bernice Glatzer Rosenthal, ed. *Nietzsche in Russia* (Princton, NJ: Princeton Un. Press, 1986), 4. About Nietzsche's influence on Lunacharsky, see Rosenthal's introduction and A. L. Tait, "Lunacharsky: a 'Nietzschean Marxist'?" in the same book, 275-292. About Lu Xun and Lunacharsky, see Lundburg, 122-126; Lu Xun, "Preface to *On Art*," in *Complete Works*, vol. 10, 294-296; Lu Xun, "Translator's note to *Art and Criticism*" in *Complete Works*, vol. 10, 298-305; Lu Xun, "Postscript to *Faust and the City*" in *Complete Works*, vol. 7, 351-361; and Lunacharsky, *Art and Criticism*, translated by Lu Xun (Shanghai: Shuimo Publisher, 1929).
⁶⁶ Lu Xun, "Postscript," *Complete Works*, vol. 10, 325-334; Lu Xun, "Translator's Note," *Complete Works*, vol. 10, 335-337.
⁶⁷ *Ibid.*
⁶⁸ *Ibid.*
⁶⁹ For Nietzsche's influence in Russia, see Bernice Glatzer Rosenthal, ed., *Nietzsche in Russia* (Princton, NJ: Princeton Un. Press, 1986); and *Nietzsche and Soviet Culture: Ally and Adversary* (Cambridge University Press, 1994).
⁷⁰ *Complete Works*, vol. 3, 356-357.
⁷¹ Lu Xun, "Preface to *Grand Series of the Chinese New Literature, Novels Series 2*," (March 2, 1935) *Complete Works*, vol. 6, 254-255.
⁷² About Lu Xun's support for the first complete translation of *Thus Spoke Zarathustra*, see Xu Fancheng, "On *Thus Spoke Zarathustra*," in No. 19, *Lu Xun Yenjiu Ziliao*, Beijing, Lu Xun Museum, 1987. For examples of Lu Xun's borrowing from *Zarathustra*, see Lu Xun, "The Night Song," *Complete Works*, vol.5, 193-194; Lu Xun, "Preface to Qiejieting Zawen," *Complete Works*, vol.6, 3-5; and Lu Xun, "From Deafness to Dumbness," *Complete Works*, vol.5, 277-279.
⁷³ Quoted from Hsia Tsi-an, *The Gate of Darkness* (Seattle: University of Washington Press, 1968), 112-113.
⁷⁴ See "Ressurection," "Gathering Edible Herbs," and "Exit from the Pass" from *Old Story Retold* [" 起死 " " 采薇 " and " 出關 "]. Also see his poem "Improvisation in the Late Fall 1935," [《亥年殘秋偶作》] in *Complete Works*, vol. 7, 451.
⁷⁵ *Historical Sources of the New Literature* [《新文學史料》] (Beijing: People's Literature Press, 1979), No. 2.
⁷⁶ Lu Xun, "On the 'Pass' of 'Exit from the Pass'" (April 30, 1936) in *Complete Works*, vol. 6, 517-521.
⁷⁷ Among the more important writings concerning Lu Xun's relations with the Zhou Yang group are Lu Xun, "An Answer to Xu Maoyong and My Views on the Issue of United Front," in *Complete Works*, vol.6, 526-544; "On the Status Quo of our Literary Movement," *Complete Works*, vol.6, 590-592; "A Response to the Letter from

Troskyites," *Complete Works*, vol., 586-589; and "A Small Collection in the Mid-Summer," *Complete Works,* vol.6, 595-598.

[78] Lu Xun, "A Small Collection in the Mid-Summer," in *Complete Works*, vol. 6, 595-598. The translation is based on *Selected Writings*, trans by Xianyi Yang and Gladys Yang, vol. 4, 303.

CHAPTER 5

Mao Zedong's Nietzsche Complex

Mao Zedong had a fancy for philosophy. Of all his own writings he was especially proud of the two essays on philosophy he wrote during WWII. As leader of the People's Republic of China, he seemed to consider himself a "philosopher king" rather than any other type of ruler. In the 1960s he welcomed Bertrand Russell (1872–1970) and Jean-Paul Sartre (1905–1980) to be his guests, an honor usually extended only to foreign heads of state or communist party chiefs. During the Cultural Revolution when his supporters hailed him "great leader, great mentor, great commander-in-chief, and great helmsman," he told a foreign visitor that he did not like such flattering designations but added that he had no objection to be called a "mentor," for he used to be a "mentor" when he was young. Towards the end of his life, he urged more often that all Chinese study philosophy, hoping it would lead to a better appreciation of his own ideas—collectively known as the "Thought of Mao Zedong."

Mao Zedong was interested in philosophy when he was a student. What remains of his homework, reading notes, correspondence, and a few published essays of the 1910s reveal a mind keen for philosophical issues. He excelled in his understanding of Chinese classics and he was eager to learn about foreign ideas. One of the Western thinkers he held in high esteem was Friedrich Nietzsche. Mao Zedong had probably mentioned Nietzsche only once in his lifetime. But that single reference, when examined in its historical contexts and traced to its sources, offers a wealth of information on Mao Zedong's approach to foreign ideas and his way of thinking in general.

In the summer of 1919 many Chinese felt betrayed after learning that the Paris Peace Conference had decided to turn over former German concessions in China to Japan, despite the fact that China had supported the Allies' war efforts. Following a violent student demonstration in Beijing on May Fourth, a wave of mass protests swept the country. On June 14 Mao Zedong launched a political journal—the *Review of the Xiangjiang River* in Changsha, the provincial capital of Hunan. His writings in the journal reflected the general mood of the time, but they also distinguished Mao Zedong from most of his contemporaries.

Chen Duxiu and other leading intellectuals had viewed the Western Allies as a moral force that would bring imperialism to an end. When their hope was dashed at the Paris Peace Conference, their sympathy was shifted from the West to Bolshevik Russia, which they saw as the champion of social and international justice. In contrast young Mao Zedong had been sympathetic to Germany. He was not so much concerned with the moral aspect of the international order as with the issue of power. He admired Otto von Bismarck and William II for their roles in making Germany a powerful nation that was strong enough to challenge the established international power structure. Mao Zedong had been nicknamed Moltke by his classmates, partly because of his sympathy for Germany, partly because he appeared to share the same family name with Helmuth Karl von Moltke (1848-1916), chief of the German general staff at the outbreak of WWI, whose name, when transliterated into Chinese, was "Mao Qi" [毛奇].[1] The peace settlement in 1919 did not disillusion him, rather, it confirmed his belief that history was not determined by moral principles but by power relations alone.

In the summer of 1919, unlike Chen Duxiu and other leftist intellectuals, Mao Zedong was more concerned with the fate of Germany than with Bolshevik Russia. In the first issue of his new journal, Mao Zedong asserted that the Western powers had created new nations in Europe in order to cripple Germany and they had no respect for the principle of national self-determination at all, as demonstrated in their snubbing the Zionists and the Korean nationalists. In the second issue of *Review of the Xiangjiang River*, he lashed out at the Versailles system and predicted its eventual collapse:

> The German nation has recently been nurtured by the philosophic ideas of Nietzsche, Fichte, Kidd, and Paulsen, such as "striving toward noble goals" or

---

* The Xiangjiang is the main river and emblem of Hunan, Mao Zedong's home province. At the time Mao Zedong was promoting provincial autonomy, hoping it would lead to a national revival.

"activism." Full of energy and vitality, it is just biding its time [to break the Versailles system].

Once set free from the Versailles system, predicted Mao Zedong, Germany would rise as a power that resembles "a newly sharpened sword," against which the whole world could hardly defend itself. Mao Zedong predicted that the SPD majority government, greatly weakened after signing the Versailles treaty, would not be able to put down another uprising and it would be replaced by a communist government. A communist Germany would then ally itself with its eastern neighbors—Austria, Czechoslovakia, Hungary and Russia, four countries where the communists had already seized power or, in Mao Zedong's view, were to seize power soon. The communist block thus created would triumph over the West in a coming "class war."[2]

Mao Zedong's reference to Nietzsche was associated with both his admiration for Germany and his identification with the communist movement. But he did not seem to know much about either Germany or communism. For instance, he did not even mention the name of Karl Marx in his essay. None of the four writers he referred to were sympathetic to communism. Of the four only Nietzsche could be counted as a recent influence in Germany. Fichte belonged more to a bygone era. Kidd was not a German but a British writer who enjoyed no popularity in Germany.* Paulsen was indeed a prestigious scholar, but he could hardly be counted as someone who had "nurtured" the German consciousness. Besides, the four writers held such diverse views that they are unlikely to be treated as a group by any one who knows Western intellectual history. Mao Zedong seems to be confused about what he was saying.

Considering the general status of Chinese understanding of Western ideas, one must not regard young Mao Zedong as a particularly irresponsible writer. Besides, one needs to take into account the fact that Mao Zedong had been disadvantaged in education during his childhood and adolescence. Mao Zedong was born in Hunan in 1893. His father, a rich farmer and merchant with little education himself, expected him to inherit his business, therefore considering learning anything beyond basic writing and calculating a waste of money. After sending Mao Zedong to study Confucian classics from village tutors for only four years, he made the thirteen-year-old boy do farm work at home. Young Mao Zedong resented

---

* Benjamin Kidd is discussed in Chapter One.

the role his father had assigned him to. After working at home for three years between 1906 and 1909, he persuaded his father to allow him to continue his study with village tutors. A year later, at the age of seventeen, he left his home village and enrolled in a primary school in a neighboring county, sitting in a class among much younger students. In 1911 he moved to Changsha and, for the next two years, enrolled in secondary schools there intermittently. During this period, he spent a few months studying on his own in Hunan Provincial Library, where he was overjoyed at the large book collection and he, as he later recalled, "greedily read books, just like a cow breaking into a neighbor's garden and feasting on its vegetables."[3] In 1913 Mao Zedong was admitted into the Provincial Fourth Normal School, which was soon merged with the First Normal School. The five years he spent in the school (1913-1918) were the only formal education he had ever completed in his lifetime.

In 1919 when Mao Zedong made his comments about the Versailles Treaty, none of Nietzsche's works had been made available in Chinese yet. Mao Zedong must have read about Nietzsche in the journal *New Youth*, to which he had been a devoted reader. In addition to Chen Duxiu's references to Nietzsche, the journal carried other writers' comments as well. In May 1918, for instance, Lin Shuang contributed an essay to it, characterizing the Great War as "Nietzsche's religion in action."[4] A few months later, an essay by Cai Yuanpei appeared in the journal, proclaiming that the state policies of Germany, Bolshevik Russia and the Western Allies were respectively based on the philosophies of Nietzsche, Tolstoi and Kropotkin.[5] All these writings could have influenced Mao Zedong's view on Nietzsche, but they did not associate Nietzsche with socialism and with such figures as Fichte, Kidd, and Paulsen.

There is no evidence that Mao Zedong knew anything about Fichte's philosophical and aesthetic theories. He may have learned about Fichte's role in arousing German nationalism from Liang Qichao or from some history primers.* The German situation in 1919 must have appeared to Mao Zedong to be similar to that in the Napoleonic era. He brought up the name of Fichte only to express his faith in a German national revival.

The fact that Mao Zedong mentioned Benjamin Kidd along with Nietzsche points to an essay written by Liang Qichao. Kidd was known to

---

* Liang Qichao, in his effort to promote nationalism in China, had introduced a number of foreign nationalist figures, including Fichte, to Chinese readers in the early 1900s.

Chinese readers as early as 1899 through a missionary publication, but he was not associated with Nietzsche until Liang Qichao wrote his essay "Kidd—a Revolutionary of the Theory of Evolution" in 1902.* Liang Qichao, however, had not mistaken Kidd for a German writer or someone having a particular impact on Germany. Due to the fact that the Chinese transliteration of the name Kidd [頡 德] includes a character that also means Germany, Mao Zedong must have mistaken Kidd for a German through a blur of memory and jumped to the conclusion that Kidd had something to do with shaping the German consciousness.

In his 1902 essay Liang Qichao presented Kidd as the latest and greatest social Darwinist thinker in an era dominated by the theory of evolution. He also characterized Nietzsche as an "individualist" and "an extremist advocate of the right of the strong," therefore another social Darwinist thinker. The distinction Liang Qichao made between Kidd and Nietzsche was obviously missed by Mao Zedong. For Mao Zedong, both Kidd and Nietzsche represented the same kind of social Darwinism advocated by Liang Qichao (and Yan Fu)—a reverse social Darwinism that aimed at empowering the oppressed people.†

Mao Zedong fully embraced Liang Qichao's idea that the established power structure could be challenged effectively only by a counter power. He, however, went beyond his predecessor's elitist agenda of "people's renovation" and added a new dimension to the reverse social Darwinism. Influenced by the Bolshevik revolution, he called for the formation of a new "power" through the union of all the oppressed masses in order to resist those "powers" that were responsible for injustice in China and in the world.⁶ It was this revolutionary reverse social Darwinism that was in his mind when he talked about the German nation being nurtured by the ideas of Nietzsche and Kidd.

From the same 1902 essay by Liang Qichao Mao Zedong must have learned that Karl Marx was a champion for the "majority of the weak," an opposite of Nietzsche.‡ It seems that Mao Zedong had taken such characterization at its face value. He did not mentioned Marx because he did not see Marx fit in a group that includes Kidd and Nietzsche. It was only

---

* See Chapter 1.

† See p. 6 and p. 8.

‡ See p. 1

later that Mao Zedong realized that his own idea of the union of all oppressed people could be traced from the Bolshevik Revolution to Marx rather than to Nietzsche and Kidd.

Mao Zedong did not mention Paulsen along with Nietzsche by accident. Paulsen was one of the Western writers he had known quite well. In late 1917 and early 1918, as a student in the First Normal School, Mao Zedong read Paulsen's *System of Ethics* as an assignment for an ethics course. The copy of the book young Mao Zedong used then has miraculously survived.* Judging from the extensive notes he wrote on its pages, the book apparently had a major influence on him. Paulsen's book offers clues to how Mao Zedong was able to fit Paulsen, Nietzsche and socialism (or communism) in the same picture in his 1919 essay.

The Chinese version of Paulsen's *System of Ethics* was published in 1909. Its translator, Cai Yuanpei, had been studying in Leipzig since 1907. Before he was sent to Germany, he had spent a few years in Japan. It is obvious that at the time he translated Paulsen's book, he was still more comfortable with Japanese than with German. He based his translation not on the German original but on a Japanese translation. The Japanese translation, in its turn, happened to be a partial translation of the English version by Frank Thilly.[7] Something must have gone wrong in the process of retranslating: the Paulsen Mao Zedong and his classmates read was very different from the original Paulsen.

Friedrich Paulsen, a well-known German philosopher at the turn of the century, was not a fan of Nietzsche. In Book One of the *System of Ethics* Paulsen expressed his concern that Nietzsche had cast an evil spell over his German contemporaries, especially the young. He wanted to roll back the "moral nihilism" represented by Nietzsche (and the "pessimism"

---

* There are two conflicting stories about how the book has survived. According to one source, when the Nationalists began to purge the Communists in 1927, Mao Zedong's relatives burned most of his diaries, class notes and books he had kept at his parents' house. Only Paulsen's book and a notebook were rescued by a friend. See Li Rui, *Comrade Mao Zedong's Early Revolutionary Activities* (Beijing: Chinese Youth Press, 1957) [李銳，《毛澤東同志的初期革命活動》北京: 人民出版社], 37-42. According to another source, one of his classmates borrowed the book from Mao Zedong and kept it for many years before he returned it to Mao Zedong in 1950. See Gao Jucun and others, *Young Mao Zedong* (Beijing: Publisher for Historical Sources of the Chinese Communist Party, 1990), 48-49.

represented by Schopenhauer) and restore to Europe its old values. Paulsen believed in a synthesis of Hellenic humanism and Christian piety, two sets of values which, in his opinion, had been rejected by Nietzsche as "ascetic ideals."

These views are not to be found in the Chinese version which covers only the "Introduction" and "Book Two" of the original book. Paulsen, however, briefly mentioned Nietzsche in the "Introduction" when he attacked cultural nihilism and a misguided Enlightenment:

> The present is characterized by a strong desire to reject *a priori* all the old accepted truths. There are many symptoms of this desire: think of the avidity with which Friedrich Nietzsche's oracular utterances concerning the necessary transformation of all values (*die Umwertung aller Werte*) are received by the young, as well as of the violent condemnation by the social democracy of all existing political and social institutions. A passionate mania for the new and unheard-of, in thought, in morals, and in modes of life, has taken hold of our times. It is utterly useless to appeal to authority and tradition; this mania is nothing but an outbreak of free individual thought, which has been repressed so long, and made distrustful by coercion; it is the reaction against the school, which forced men not to think, but to memorize, against the church, which asked them not to think, but to believe. These are the symptoms of the *Aufklärung*, the *Aufklärung* which was long since reported dead; it has come back to life and has taken hold of the masses, of the young men especially, of course; they want to do their own thinking and mold their own lives, and not to be governed blindly by the traditional thoughts and actions of others. And to this they have a perfect right.... It will be the business of ethics to invite the doubter and the inquirer to assist in the common effort to discover fixed principles which shall help the judgment to understand the aims and problems of life.... Perhaps he will then find that much of what he was about to cast aside, as a mere command of caprice, is rooted in the very nature of things, and consequently also in his own will.[8]

It is hard to image what would have been Mao Zedong's response if these words had been correctly translated into Chinese. What Mao Zedong and his classmates read was the Chinese version that had turned Paulsen's scathing remarks on Nietzsche, socialism, the youth culture, the Enlightenment, and cultural nihilism into jubilant cheers:

> The contemporary social mind has an increasing tendency to seek what is new, to reject the old accepted *a priori* truths. There are many evidences of this tendency, such as the statements of Nietzsche, the view of the age of youth that everything should be transformed, of socialism that would change the old customs of state and society. These are but the most obvious examples. The contemporary age, whether in thought, in morality, or in life styles, is rejecting

all things old and seeking the new. As for the authority of religion and its ancient proverbs, everyone regards them as worthless. Having been so excessively repressed, in reaction they rebel and become skeptics, and their subjective ideas are breaking down the walls and escaping in all directions, in reaction to the old unthinking learning and the religions of unquestioning faith. [Mao's marginal note: **All our nation's two thousand years of scholarship may be said to be unthinking learning.**] These are the characteristics of the Enlightenment. The Enlightenment of the past still exists and is reappearing again today. At first taking hold of the young people, today it is spreading among the common people. [Mao's marginal note: **This is today's situation in our nation.**] Those who have been oppressed by the thought and the prescriptions for living of the past, regard this as the blind leading the blind, and inevitably want to do their own thinking and to open up another world. Such is the right of freedom. Free thought, free living is the first right of human life and the first duty. The most precious quality of the realm of the spirit is none other than independence. Independence of the spirit lies in the freedom to think, not in relying on ready-made beliefs. The problem of ethics is to help those who have fallen into skepticism, to discover the true purpose and task of life and to give it a foundation in free investigation.[9]

Mao Zedong never had a chance to know the original Paulsen, who was a traditionalist at heart. It was the Chinese Paulsen who inspired him to condemn China's "two thousand years of scholarship." It was also this Chinese Paulsen who appeared to be allied with Nietzsche, socialism, and cultural nihilism. Such a problematic understanding of Paulsen and Nietzsche formed another aspect of Mao Zedong's Nietzsche complex that was manifested in his essay on the Versailles Treaty.

If Mao Zedong had only minimal and erroneous knowledge of Western ideas, he was the rule rather than an exception of his time. In his search for Western ideas, Mao Zedong was handicapped by historical limitations which his generation of Chinese intellectuals could not surmount. There was a tragic-comic element in young Mao Zedong's pursuit of philosophy. In 1920 he admitted to his friends that he did not have "a clear idea about all those 'isms' and theories" and he announced a plan to spend the next two years to "assimilate the essentials of all theories, ancient and modern, Chinese and foreign" by reading translations and journal articles and, possibly, to write a book on philosophy.[10] Already deeply involved in provincial politics and in the nascent communist movement, he did not have a chance to carry out his two-year plan for philosophy.

Mao Zedong would never have succeeded as a CCP activist if he had only learned oversimplified and distorted foreign ideas from sources such as

Liang Qichao, Cai Yuanpei, or Chen Duxiu. Fortunately during his student years he had also read many Chinese classical works of philosophy and history, of which he often demonstrated profound understanding. Between 1921 and 1927 when the newly founded CCP was closely directed by Comintern representatives, Mao Zedong, as one of the party's leading members, had acquired firsthand knowledge of Leninist tactics and organizational skills and learned some basic theories of Marxism. Since Zhu De and Mao Zedong had founded the Chinese Red Army in 1927, they were left on their own to keep the CCP movement alive in China's remote rural areas. It was then that Mao Zedong, drawing on age-old precedents and ideas from China's past as well as the Russian experiences, had gradually created and perfected effective political and military strategies for the Chinese revolution. With these strategies Mao Zedong made significant contribution to the Chinese Resistance during WWII and led the CCP to victory in the civil war. These strategies have proved to be the most important part of the "Thought of Mao Zedong."

Along with these creative ideas that grew out of his thorough knowledge of Chinese history and his experiences as a revolutionary leader, the "Thought of Mao Zedong" also includes foreign ideas that Mao Zedong had learned from specious sources and in specious ways. Mao Zedong resorted to such foreign ideas when he confronted problems which had no precedents in Chinese history, such as issues related to industrialization and other aspects of modern society. On such occasions, when creative borrowing of foreign ideas and foreign experiences were of critical importance, the intuitive and simplistic approach Mao Zedong had inherited from Liang Qichao, Cai Yuanpei, and Chen Duxiu proved to be inadequate and disastrous. For example, Mao Zedong's knowledge about economy did not go beyond what he had learned from a few articles by Marx, Engels and Lenin and one textbook on political economy published in the Soviet Union, he made the decision to eliminate market economy and speed up collectivization, believing that China could thus be catapulted into communism. Another example was his call for increasing China's steel output through building backyard furnaces across the country. The whole policy was based on a vague idea that a nation's industrial strength was in some way correlated to its steel output. There are parallels between these childish policies and the way Chinese intellectuals treated Nietzsche and other Western thinkers in early twentieth century. The historical contexts were different, but the same attitude and approach to foreign ideas were in function. If distorting Nietzsche seems to be an innocent academic flaw, misconceived policies could and did cause suffering to millions of people.

Although Mao Zedong no longer talked about Nietzsche after 1919, he had not outgrown his Kidd-Nietzsche complex and Paulsen-Nietzsche complex. He held on to them and gave them new expressions. In a debate with his friends in January 1921, Mao Zedong argued that "human life consists of nothing but ever growing material desires," therefore the capitalists cannot be educated to accept a new society. The only way to effect social transformation is to overcome the resistance of capitalists with a greater power.[11] This was the same reverse social Darwinism Mao Zedong had learned from Yan Fu and Liang Qichao and associated with Kidd and Nietzsche. He repeated the same idea for the rest of his life, mainly using the language of class struggle. To perceive the world purely in terms of power relations may appear reasonable to a revolutionary leader who had to fight for his party's survival and to lead it to power, it is nonetheless a one-sided and crude perception, a social Darwinist perception shared by reverse social Darwinists. Its absurdity became apparent when Mao Zedong, as leader of the PRC, began to apply it to the CCP's leadership circle and to the Chinese society at large. It had poisoned political life and cultural life in the Mao Zedong era.

The iconoclastic sentiment and cultural nihilism associated with Paulsen and Nietzsche also remained with Mao Zedong, sometimes latent, other times apparent. It took on a monstrous form during the "Great Proletarian Cultural Revolution" when Mao Zedong called for smashing all things "feudal," "capitalist," and "revisionist," meaning all cultural influences from China, the West, and the Soviet block. As the most powerful man in China at the time, Mao Zedong was able to put into practice on a grand scale some Nietzschean ideas he had acquired from dubious sources nearly half a century ago.

The last years of Mao Zedong was a tragedy both for himself and for China. The old chairman had been instrumental in creating conditions that make the study of Western thought possible in China.* But he himself was trapped in a bygone era, unable to go beyond the simplistic approach in regard to foreign ideas. Toward the end of his life, while still believing himself to be true to the spirit of Marxism, he became increasingly aware of his indebtedness to China's past. It resulted in a new synthesis of things

---

* See Chapter 8, from p. 117 on.

foreign and Chinese, one different from those political and military strategies he had created before 1949. It was a vision of an egalitarian society, predominantly agricultural, maintained according to Legalist political tradition, continually energized and renewed by class struggles. In such a vision, one can still recognize the marks of his Kidd-Nietzsche complex and Paulsen-Nietzsche complex.

Notes

[1] Siao Yu, *Mao Tse-tung and I were Beggars* (Syracuse University, 1959), 69-70; Zhongguo Geming Bowuguan and Hunan Sheng Bowuguan, eds., *Sources of the Study Society of People's Renovation* (Beijing: People Press, 1980) [中國革命博物館，湖南博物館，《新民學會資料》], 250; also see Schram, *Mao's Road to Power* (New York: Columbia University Press, 1992), 248-249.

[2] Mao Zedong, "The agony of the Germans in signing the [Versailles] Treaty" [德意志人的沉痛簽約], *Review of the Xiangjiang River* [湘江評論], No. 2 (July 21, 1919). From *Supplement to Collected Works of Mao Zedong* [《毛澤東集補集》] (Tokyo: Sososha, 1983), vol. 1, 83-93.

[3] Gao Jucun, Chen Feng, Tang Zhennan and Tian Yuliang, *Young Mao Zedong* (Beijing: Publisher for Historical Sources of the Chinese Communist Party, 1990) [高菊村，陳峰，唐振南，田余糧,《青年毛澤東》北京: 中共黨史資料出版社]), 24.

[4] Ling Shuang, "The Religion of German philosopher Nietzsche [凌霜，"德意志哲學家尼采的宗教"]," *New Youth*, vol. 4, no. 5 (May 15, 1918): 437-441. The essay was based on an American author's book review of William M. Satler's *Nietzsche the Thinker*.

[5] Cai Yuanpei, "The Great War in Europe and Philosophy" [蔡元培，"歐戰與哲學"]. Originally published in *New Trend* [《新潮》], vol. 1, no. 1 (December 1918) and reprinted in *The Orient* [《東方雜誌》], vol. 16, no. 1 and *New Youth*, vol. 5, no. 5. Cited from Cai Yuanpei, *Selected Works of Cai Yuanpei* (Beijing: People's Press, 1984), 25-31.

[6] Mao Zedong, "The Great Union of the Masses," ["民眾的大聯合"], from Mao Zedong, *Colleted Writings of Mao Zedong* [《毛澤東集》] (Tokyo: Sososha, 1972), vol. 1, 57-69.

[7] Friedrich Paulsen, *System der Ethik mit einem Umriss der Staats und Gesellschaftslehre* (Berlin: Hertz, 1889); Friedrich Paulsen, *A System of Ethics*, trans. by Frank Thilly, (New York: Scribner's Sons, 1899). I have not found the Japanese edition on which the Chinese translation was based. The Chinese translation by Cai Yuanpei, along with Mao Zedong's notes have been translated into English by Stuard R. Schram, see his *Mao's Road to Power: Revolutionary Writings 1912-1949* (New York: Columbia

University Press, 1992). Dr. Schram discussed the background of the book in its introduction, see page xxix.

[8] Thilly's English translation is used here. See Paulsen, 1899, 28-29.

[9] Schram, 1992, 193-194.

[10] The Museum of the Chinese Revolution and the Museum of Hunan, ed. *Sources of the People's Renovation* (Beijing: People's Press, 1980), p. 33 and p.64.

[11] *Ibid*.: 149-150.

CHAPTER 6

Li Shicen:

Nietzsche versus Chinese Traditions

There were similarities between Li Shicen and Mao Zedong in their early lives. Li Shicen was born in a village in Hunan not far from that of Mao Zedong. He was Mao Zedong's senior by one year minus one day. Just like Mao Zedong, he was taught by village tutors and then moved to Changsha, the provincial capital, to continue his education. Later he also went to a normal school, though not the same one in Changsha, but the Tokyo Advanced Normal School in Japan. As a student, he was also keenly interested in philosophy, especially in Nietzsche. There may have been a friendship between Li Shicen and Mao Zedong. Li Shicen was once invited, through Mao Zedong's arrangement, to give a speech at the First Normal School. After the event, he and his hosts went to swim in the Xiangjiang River and he taught Mao Zedong and others how to swim in Western-style kicks and strokes which he had learned in Japan.[1] The two men's paths diverged after they left school. While Mao Zedong went into politics and later became the leader of the Chinese communist movement, Li Shicen devoted himself to the study of Western ideas and played a major role in introducing Western ideas to Chinese readers.

Li Shicen had written about many Western philosophers, such as Henri Bergson, William James, Sören Kierkegaard, Bertrand Russell, John Dewey, Edmund Husserl, and others. But before his turning to Marxism in the last few years of his life, he had shown an enduring interest in Nietzsche rather than in anyone else. When he was a student in Japan, he later remembered, he was "greatly inspired" by the German philosopher and reading Nietzsche made his life "full of colors."[2] In 1920, after he returned to China and became editor in chief of the journal *People's Bell*, he compiled a special issue of the journal to feature Nietzsche, to which he himself contributed an essay and a bibliography.[3] In the same year he also delivered a lecture on Nietzsche in Changsha, Hunan.[4] Over the next few years he continued to be interested in Nietzsche and in 1931 he published *A Brief Introduction to the Superman Philosophy*, the first booklet on Nietzsche in China.[5]

Li Shicen's writings on Nietzsche have some obvious defects. They are mostly informal and spontaneous, with minimal documentation. The fact that there are little textual analysis indicates that they are based on secondary sources rather than on original works of Nietzsche. Besides, the Nietzsche portrayed by Li Shicen seems to be too consistent and clear-cut to resemble the German dialectical thinker. Nevertheless, compared with most other writers discussed so far in the current book, Li Shicen was better trained in philosophy and he brought the discussion of Nietzsche's philosophy in China to a more sophisticated level.

Many Chinese writers before Li Shicen had associated Nietzsche with the Darwinian theory of evolution and social Darwinism. Li Shicen emphatically rejected such an association. In his view Nietzsche's philosophy differed diametrically from the Darwinian theory or social Darwinism. First, according to Nietzsche, life consists of constant conquering and creating. Its underlying drive is the "will to power," instead of the Darwinian "struggle for life." Second, Nietzsche found that in human society the strong are often less well adapted and the weak are not necessarily unfit. He therefore did not view the "survival of the fittest" as a rule in human society. Finally, Nietzsche did not believable the theory of "natural selection" as applicable to human society because it ignores man's inner power while giving undue emphasis to external factors. Li Shicen believed that the Darwinian theory of evolution or social Darwinism induces man to adapt himself to his environment while Nietzsche's philosophy encourages man to uplift his life by conquering and creating his environment.[6]

Li Shicen approached the idea of superman in a non-Darwinian manner. In "Nietzsche's View of Evolution," a chapter from his 1931 book, he quoted from *Thus Spoke Zarathustra*:

> I teach you the superman. Man is something that shall be overcome. What have you done to overcome him?

> All beings so far have created something beyond themselves; and do you want to be the ebb of this great flood and even go back to the beasts rather than overcome man? What is the ape to man? A laughingstock or a painful embarrassment. And man shall be just that for the superman: a laughingstock or a painful embarrassment. You have made your way from worm to man, and much in you is still worm. Once you were apes, even now, too, man is more ape than any ape.[7]

Li Shicen viewed phrases such as "from worm to man" to be "symbolic expressions" used "for the convenience of presentation." He emphasized that "superman is not a new species evolved from man through evolution, as man was from ape."[8]

Li Shicen found three layers of meaning in the concept of "superman." Nietzsche, wrote Li Shicen, regarded the "will to power" as mankind's "true self," from which arise all material and spiritual movements in history. In the process of mankind's "unrestricted unfolding of the true self" some individuals who live by the will to power could not help having "a sense of distance" from the others who are left behind due to their lack of the will to power. This "sense of distance," explained Li Shicen, was the first definition of superman. Second, superman should not be viewed as the ultimate goal of evolution but as a "milestone on the road of evolution"— another definition of superman. Thirdly, since mankind regains its freedom through superman, superman is "the symbol of mankind's salvation"— Li Shicen's third definition of superman.[9] Even if Li Shicen had not fully grasped the meaning of "superman," by defining superman as "a sense of distance," "a symbol of salvation," and "a milestone," instead of a new species, he had at least rescued Nietzsche from the vulgar hands of Darwinists.

While not a Darwinist, Li Shicen had faith in man's evolution, or in the idea of progress. He tried three approaches to reconcile the concept of eternal recurrence and the idea of evolution. The first was to make a distinction between the quantity and the quality of the "will to power." In terms of its quantity, eternal recurrence should be considered an undeniable fact:

> In its totality, the universe is a monster of power, that has neither beginning nor end, that neither decreases nor increases, that is neither mechanistic nor teleological. It is a world where incessant self-creation and incessant self-destruction elicit each other and clash with each other. Our life is the same; it is the perpetual recurrence of self-destruction and self-creation.[10]

But in a different dimension, the quality of the "will to power" is not constant—it is "in flux":

> So far as it [the will to power] is in flux, the world has a drive to move forward. Thus, although the world recurs eternally, it is not without evolution, without creation.... The will to power is the eternal recurrence of destruction and creation, but it always changes and develops. This is what the world and human life are like. Mankind always strives for a more glorious future. It will never stop in the same place.[11]

This is an awkward explanation. If the "will to power" involves constant destruction and creation, it can hardly be perceived as making progress. If it is moving in a forward or upward direction, it can hardly be described as recurring. Li Shicen seems to have realized the difficulty. He tried another strategy:

> What really motivated Nietzsche is to portray the universe as extremely lifeless and meaningless so that it can be rescued by the superman, so that the lifeless could be given life and the meaningless be given meaning.[12]

This second answer presumes a two-stage process. At the first stage, the universe is so lifeless and meaningless that it looks as if it were going to recur forever. Then superman arises and sets the universe in a progressive motion.

Probably uneasy about the idea that the universe had once been without evolution or progress, Li Shicen did not have much confidence in the second approach either. His third approach to the issue was an outright objection:

> Judging Nietzsche's thought from a logical point of view, it is, after all, a pity that Nietzsche brought in the idea of eternal recurrence into his superman philosophy.[13]

All these approaches point to Li Shicen's faith in progress, a faith so deep-rooted that he was oblivious to a more obvious approach—to acknowledge that Nietzsche did not believe in progress.

Li Shicen was not a neutral interpreter. Except for his doubt over the concept of eternal occurrence, he defended all other aspects of Nietzsche's philosophy against its critics. In his 1920 lecture, he argued that although one should embrace the idea of "equality" in terms of "external regulations," one must recognize "classes" in regard to man's inner quality. This, Li Shicen asserted, was what Nietzsche meant when he urged people to strive for higher "classes."[14] In his 1931 booklet, he went even further to show Nietzsche as a champion of lower social classes:

Nietzsche was disappointed at genius just as he was at the masses. He thought that in modern society those who are viewed as the high and the noble are mostly philistines, and those who are regarded as the lowly and worthless are mostly noble persons. Therefore those commonly known as heroes or great men are not necessarily noble, and those commonly known as the ignorant and the lowly are not necessarily ignorant and lowly. These terms such as high, noble, ignorant, and lowly should be applied to people according to the quality of their inner life, not according to their external attributes.... This is the essence of Nietzsche's aristocratism.[15]

Li Shicen and many other Chinese intellectuals who had lived and studied abroad were painfully aware of the gap between industrialized countries and their own country. Unable to understand China's backwardness in a broader historical context and to find out its many causes, they blamed it on the country's tradition and the people's mentality. In his eagerness to effect "a fundamental transformation of the Chinese national mentality" through introducing Nietzsche's philosophy, Li Shicen often compromised his philosophical judgment.[16] When writing about Nietzsche he always juxtaposed unsympathetic and faultfinding interpretations of Chinese ideas and values against sympathetic and apologetic interpretations of Nietzsche's ideas and values.

According to Li Shicen, Nietzsche, influenced by Max Stirner's concept of the "self" as "a unique, indivisible, and heterogeneous microcosm that was self-creating and self-sufficient," also refused to impose any other interest above individual interest, be it the other world, God, abstract ideas, or the interest of a class, a state or even the whole society.[17] But unlike Stirner whose social ideal was an association of egoists, each acting according to his own interests, Nietzsche was concerned with transforming man's nature, "elevating man to the status of supermen and founding a world of supermen." The point is not that a society should serve, or sacrifice itself for, the will of a few individuals, but that "humanity consists in free and genuine individuals, not anything supra-individual." Li Shicen characterized Nietzsche's individualism as a combination of "cosmopolitanism," "humanism," and "character-ennobling." [人類主義，人道主義，人格主義][18]

Li Shicen claimed that the Chinese were especially unenlightened in regard to individualism. In China, he argued, individuals used to be defined by their social roles according to the Confucian tradition. The very word "individualism," when translated into Chinese, carried a negative undertone. Taoist philosophers, on the other hand, invariably treated all social relations as detrimental to individuality. Even when some Chinese thinkers conceived of a social order based on the interest of individuals, they often treated individuals as a homogeneous whole or thought of individual interests purely in terms of material needs. Li Shicen believed that the Chinese were in dire need to appropriate Nietzsche's individualism and to accept the idea of a society founded on the private interests of separate and unique individuals.[19]

Li Shicen was more familiar with *The Birth of Tragedy* than with Nietzsche's works. He believed that Nietzsche's views on art contained an important lesson for the Chinese. He criticized the Chinese for being too much occupied with morality and knowledge. Morality and knowledge, he explained, are static by nature and therefore are toxic to anyone who has taken them in excess. The antidote to an overdose of morality and knowledge is Dionysian art, which is always in a state of flux. In Li Shicen's view, the Chinese "had never known the existence of a world of Dionysian ecstasy" and they "had done nothing but indulge in Apollonian dreams." They must learn Dionysian art as "the expression of life's climax, an intensified and passionate existence in a status of intoxication." They should know that Apollonian art, which deals with images, can be useful only when merged with Dionysian art and serves as a supplement to it.[20]

Despite his advocacy of Dionysian art, Li Shicen's ultimate concern was practical and social. He saw Dionysian art as a remedy to what he thought to be his countrymen's defects: they "were too utopian, conciliatory, and conservative" and they "had always searched for happiness and contentment in the world of ideas and sought inner peace under the aegis of Apollo." He hoped to instill the Dionysian spirit in the Chinese and transport them to the "world of will" so that they could overcome these defects and become "realistic, revolutionary, and creative."[21] His ultimate goal was social transformation. For once the Chinese were energized and ennobled by the Dionysian art, they would be able "to create a paradise on earth with a tragic spirit."[22] Li Shicen probably did not realize that in Nietzsche's theory of Greek tragedy, there is no room at all for such a vision.

In a chapter on "Nietzsche's view of morality" in his 1931 booklet, Li Shicen borrowed three ideas from Nietzsche to attack Chinese values. The first idea was the distinction Nietzsche made between "noble morality" and "slave morality." Li Shicen characterized the former as "promoting the strong and the great," and the latter as "protecting the weak and the small."[23] He asserted that Confucian virtues such as "loyalty" and "filial piety" were all moral precepts imposed on the weak to keep them weak and were "slave morality."[24]

The second idea Li Shicen borrowed from Nietzsche was Zarathustra's remark on "pity" and "love" and his call for "becoming hard."[25] Nietzsche did not like "pity," explained Li Shicen, because it "destroys independence, fortitude, perseverance and the fighting spirit of those being pitied." On the other hand, though "becoming hard" sounds cruel, it can elicit "independence, fortitude, perseverance and a fighting spirit" from others, thereby benefiting them. Li Shicen thought that the Chinese ideal of a benevolent government protecting the people was similar to Christian values and had to be abandoned.[26]

The third idea Li Shicen found relevant was based on the "spirit's three metamorphoses" from *Thus Spoke Zarathustra*. He treated the camel, the lion and the child as standing for three sets of qualities that a "warrior in life" should have. The camel stands for perseverance and endurance; the lion for courage, the skill to destroy, defiance of authorities and the ability to impose laws; the child for affirmation and optimism. It is amusing and sad to read how Li Shicen applied Nietzsche's "three metamorphoses" to his countrymen:

> The Chinese look like a camel, but it is a sick camel instead of a robust one. The Chinese look also like a lion, but it is a sleeping lion instead of an awake one. So far as the spirit of a child is concerned, the Chinese do not have a trace of it. Chinese children could only drag along with their long sleeves and their long pants. Could they ever dream of how Western children feel in their sailor suits? If Chinese children do not have children's spirit, what can we expect from those precocious youths?[27]

A Brief Introduction to Superman Philosophy was originally intended to be part of a more ambitious project, a book named *Nietzsche's Thought*. By the time the booklet was published (1931), Li Shicen's interest in Nietzsche had already waned. He translated Lange's *History of Materialism* in 1931 and soon became a Marxist. In his *Outline of Philosophy* published in 1933, he characterized Marxism as "having turned philosophy into a science of methodology" and predicted that it would have "an impressive growth in our time and in the foreseeable future."[28] To better understand this change, one can review the four main reasons he gave for writing his booklet on Nietzsche. First, Nietzsche's teaching of superman could make the "phlegmatic" Chinese more sensitive and active. Second, Nietzsche's philosophy could correct the worst failing of the Chinese nation, its tendency to compromise. Third, Nietzsche could teach the Chinese a "philosophy of rebellion." Fourth, Nietzsche's pronouncement "God is dead" could be used to criticize polytheism in China and turn the Chinese away from superstition. Having these objectives in mind, it is only natural that he would turn from Nietzsche to Marx. Marx's philosophy must appear to him unequivocally invigorating, uncompromising, rebellious and atheistic. Besides, it called for a revolution that was consciously or unconsciously wished for by all those like Li Shicen. Li Shicen had referred to Nietzsche's philosophy as "the best stimulant" for the Chinese people, now he seemed to have found in Marxism a stimulant better than the best.

Notes

[1] The event was recalled by a student of the First Normal School, see Gao Jucun et al, *Young Mao Zedong* (Beijing: Publisher for Historical Sources of the Chinese Communist Party, 1990), 51. The time given, spring 1918, may be incorrect, for Li Shicen did not return to China until 1920.

[2] Li Shicen, "A Confession of my Attitudes toward Life," from *Lectures of Li Shicen*, 19-20.

[3] Li Shicen, "A Criticism of Nietzsche's Thought," and "Works by and about Nietzsche" in Vol. 2 No. 1 of *People's Bell* (August 1920) [民鐸]. The essay was later reprinted in in *Essays of Li Shicen* (Shanghai: Commercial Press, 1924) [李石岑論文集].

[4] The lecture entitled "The Thought of Nietzsche and our Life" was sponsored by the General Educational Association of Hunan. It was published in *Lectures of Li Shicen* (Shanghai: Commercial Press, 1924) [李石岑演講集].

[5] Li Shicen, *A Brief Introduction to Superman Philosophy* [《超人哲學淺說》], (Shanghai: Commercial Press, 1931). The book's preface was dated 1930.

[6] Li Shicen, *Lectures*, 140.

[7] *Portable Nietzsche*, 124. Walter Kaufmann has translated the German word *Übermensch* into "overman," a rendition that has been accepted by many writers. Since Kaufmann's translation was unknown to most historical figures discussed in the current book, I will continue to use "superman," even when quoting from Kaufmann.

[8] Li Shicen, 1931, 66-67.

[9] *Ibid.*, 67-68.

[10] *Ibid.*, 50-51

[11] *Ibid.*

[12] *Ibid.*, 51-52.

[13] *Ibid.*

[14] Li Shicen, *Lectures*, 141-143.

[15] Li Shicen, *Brief Introduction*, 68-69.
[16] *Ibid.*, 1-3.
[17] *Ibid.*, 28-31.
[18] *Ibid.*, 31-32, 88-89, 90-91.
[19] *Ibid.*, 91.
[20] *Ibid.*: 93-94. Wang Guowei expressed similar opinions, see p. 22
[21] *Ibid.*, 41-43.
[22] *Ibid.*, 39-44.
[23] *Ibid.*, 72.
[24] *Ibid.*, 72-80.
[25] *Ibid.*, 73-75; *Portable Nietzsche*, 326.
[26] *Ibid.*, 72-80.
[27] *Ibid.* 79-80.
[28] Li Shicen, "An Outline of Philosophy," [哲學概論] in Yi Jianfei and Fang Songhua, *Selected Readings of Contemporary Chinese Philosophy* [懌劍飛，方忪華，《中國現代哲學原著選》] (Shanghai: Fudan University Press, 1989), 235.

CHAPTER 7

Chen Quan:

the Appropriation of Nietzsche by the Right

New and better translations of Nietzsche were published in the 1930s, often with many reprints. As Nietzsche was gaining more readers in China, those who made him popular in the previous decade had become less enthusiastic about him. Some of them had carried their Nietzschean ideas and sentiments over into the Communist movement. Others, due to the Nazi use of Nietzsche, were reluctant to talk about the German philosopher, even if they were still interested in him. From the mid 1930s on, Nietzsche's philosophy was increasingly appropriated by a few writers on the right until it was made the ideological underpinning of a pro-Fascist movement in the early 1940s. The key figure of this development was Chen Quan.

Chen Quan was born in 1905, younger than other writers discussed here previously. His formal education in Western learning appears to be quite impressive. A graduate of the Department of Western Languages and Literature at the Peking National Tsinghua University, he was sent to study at Oberlin College in the United States. After receiving both bachelor's and master's degrees there, he went on to study in Germany. He studied both literature and philosophy at the University of Cologne.

He witnessed the Nazi seizure of power in 1933. The revelry of Nazi supporters over Hitler's appointment as chancellor left a deep impression on him. At a party hosted by his landlady, he remembered later, he was filled with "shame and gratitude" when a guest toasted for a "revival" of China similar to the one going on in Germany. He also witnessed the Nazi persecution of the Jews. His own professor was first attacked in newspapers and then discharged from his university position for having a Jewish mother and a Jewish wife. But this tragic event had an unexpected effect on him. He remembered the professor telling him:

> The authorities must have their reasons [for persecuting him]. If only the nation can be free, it does not matter for an individual to make sacrifices. Germany can mistreat me, but it can not stop me from loving it from the bottom of my heart.

The professor asked him "not to portray too dark a picture of Germany" when he returned to China.[1]

Chen Quan left Germany for China and soon became a professor at the National Wuhan University and, later, at the National Tsinghua University. His first major publication, "From Schopenhauer to Nietzsche," appeared in the *Tsinghua Journal* in April 1936, an article running more than fifty pages, documented and with a bibliography that includes both German and English sources. With Li Shicen dead for two years, Lu Xun having only about half a year to live, and other prominent writers keeping silent about Nietzsche, Chen Quan came to be seen as the leading authority on Nietzsche's philosophy in China.

The title of the article "From Schopenhauer to Nietzsche" is misleading. The article is neither a comparative study of the two German philosophers, nor a survey of part of German philosophical history. Its subject is Nietzsche's intellectual development, which was divided by its author into three periods according to Nietzsche's changing attitudes towards Schopenhauer: the "period of agreement," the "period of transition," and the "period of negation."

Based on two of Nietzsche's early works, *The Birth of Tragedy* and "Schopenhauer as Educator" in *Untimely Meditations*, Chen Quan argued that there was a "period of agreement" when Nietzsche inherited Schopenhauer's pessimism. It is a difficult case to make. Nietzsche himself characterized *The Birth of Tragedy* as expressing "by means of Schopenhauerian and Kantian formulas strange and new valuations which were basically at odds with Kant's and Schopenhauer's spirit and taste."[2] In his "Schopenhauer as Educator" Nietzsche did not focus on Schopenhauer's pessimism but on his integrity and courage as a philosopher and man. Of course, scholars are entitled to alternative interpretations of these two early works of Nietzsche. The problem with Chen Quan is that he misunderstood almost everything Nietzsche said in the two books.

Chen Quan wrote that the early Nietzsche attached great significance to the cult of Dionysus which enabled the Greeks to "eliminate individuals" through "intoxication."³ This was a misrepresentation of *The Birth of Tragedy* in which Nietzsche talked about the "collapse of the principle of individuation," a reference to a mystic "primordial union," a union between man and man, and between man and nature, in the intensity of Dionysian ecstasy.⁴ The "collapse of the principle of individuation" is a blissful experience and does not lead to philosophical pessimism, as Chen Quan believed.

Chen Quan maintained that, in the "period of agreement," Nietzsche had already some reservations about Schopenhauer's pessimism:

> In *The Birth of Tragedy,* Nietzsche told us that the world of suffering is in dire need for the art of tragedy. Only through the art of tragedy, can an individual have illusory images of release, can he immerse himself in observing these illusory images, as if sitting peacefully in a boat, swaying in the sea.... It is unlikely that Schopenhauer himself would have agreed to such a modification and interpretation of his philosophy.⁵

What Chen Quan alleged to be Nietzsche's opinion turns out to be Schopenhauer's own words. Nietzsche was merely quoting Schopenhauer to elucidate the concept of the Apollonian:

> We might apply to Apollo the words of Schopenhauer when he speaks of the man wrapped in the veil of *maya*: 'just as in a stormy sea that, unbounded in all directions, raises and drops, mountainous waves, howling, a sailor sits in a boat and trusts in his frail bark: so in the midst of a world of torments the individual human being sits quietly, supported by and trusting in the principle of individuation.'⁶

It is obvious that Chen Quan understood neither Greek tragedy nor the concept of the Apollonian.

According to Chen Quan, Nietzsche characterized Schopenhauer's "ideal man" in the following words:

> He is always ready to be the first to sacrifice himself for the sake of truth, though being fully aware that truth carries the seeds of suffering. Certainly his courage will destroy his worldly happiness. He must hate the mankind he loves and the society from which he has come. He must destroy those men and things without mercy, even though he feels sorrow for them. He will be misunderstood. He will be regarded as a comrade to the forces which he loathes. The masses will consider his opinions wrong. But he must fight for justice.

These words, in Chen Quan's view, have too little pessimism to "be compatible with Schopenhauer's beliefs."⁷

The passage, actually, was a distorted translation and was quoted out of context. The original text was intended to show the difference between a

"Schopenhauerian human being" and the "so-called scholarly human being" in respect to "truthfulness":

> [A Schopenhauerean man] strangely composed about himself and his own welfare, in his knowledge full of blazing, consuming fire and far removed from the cold and contemptible neutrality of the so-called scientific man, exalted high above all sullen and ill-humoured reflection, always offering himself as the first sacrifice to the perceived truth and permeated with the awareness of what sufferings must spring from his truthfulness. He will, to be sure, destroy his earthly happiness through his courage... but he may console himself with the words once employed by his great teacher, Schopenhauer: "A happy life is impossible: the highest that man can attain is a *heroic one*. He leads it who, in whatever shape or form, struggles against great difficulties for something that is to the benefit of all and in the end is victorious, but who is ill-rewarded for it or not rewarded at all.... He is remembered and is celebrated as a hero; his will, mortified a whole life long by effort and labour, ill success and the world's ingratitude, is extinguished in Nirvana."[8]

It seems that Chen Quan's problem was not only his inability to grasp the text but also his lack of imagination—he could not imagine a philosophical pessimism that goes hand in hand with heroism.

Chen Quan thought *Human, All Too Human* signaled the beginning of Nietzsche's "period of transition." Nietzsche, Chen Quan believed, had gradually realized the "danger of relying on tragedy and Schopenhauer's pessimism" and recognized that Wagner's music could only serve as a "narcotic" that makes people oblivious of their suffering temporarily. Therefore he rejected metaphysics and art, and turned to science:

> Nietzsche asked us to observe life objectively, precisely, and scientifically, undisturbed by any emotion, unrestrained in any way and making no assumption. Put differently, he asked us not to take any stand. This stand of no stand is Nietzsche's new stand.

Chen Quan maintained that it was Nietzsche's opinion that, relying on science, people could "avoid taking responsibilities" and "throw off the restraints of conscience.... because the sting of conscience is a stupidity just like a dog nibbling at a brick."[9]

In *Human all Too Human*, as part of his "logical world-denial," Nietzsche revealed a positivistic tendency in his approach to certain issues. However he did not renounce art and he was wary of the dominance of science:

> But if science provides us with less and less pleasure, and deprives us of more and more pleasure through casting suspicion on the consolations of metaphysics,

religion and art, then that mightiest source of joy to which mankind owes almost all its humanity will become impoverished. For this reason a higher culture must give man a double-brain, as it were two brain-ventricles, one for the perceptions of science, the other for those of non-science: lying beside one another, not confused together, separable, capable of being shut off; this is a demand of health.[10]

Nor did Nietzsche ask people to shun responsibilities or abandon conscience in *Human, All Too Human*. He suggested that people examine the ground on which responsibilities are based. He called the "sting of conscience" "a piece of stupidity," but added, "In every case in which a thing is done with 'because' and 'why', man acts *without* conscience; but not yet for that reason against it."[11] So again Chen Quan's conclusion was based on misreading.

The "period of transition" was followed by the "period of negation" in which, according to Chen Quan, Nietzsche had finally walked out of the shadow of Schopenhauer's pessimism and founded a life-affirming philosophy. Chen Quan traced the origin of the concept of the "will to power" to three passages from *The Gay Science*. The first of the three describes the characteristics of life:

> *What is life?* Life—that is continually shedding something that wants to die. Life—that is: being cruel and inexorable against everything about us that is growing old and weak—and not only about *us*. Life—that is, then, being without reverence for those who are dying, who are wretched, who are ancient? Constantly being a murderer? —And yet old Moses said: 'Thou shalt not kill.'[12]
> [Translated by Walter Kaufmann]

This is a provocative statement but it is open to non-literal interpretation. Chen Quan, through mistranslation, made it sound unequivocally cruel:

> What is life? Life—that is pushing aside the dying thing constantly. Life—that is battling the weak and the old among us, and not merely among us, without mercy. Life—that is to battle the dying, the wretched and the old, showing them no reverence? Constantly being a murderer?[13]

The second passage from *The Gay Science* was based on a Heraclitean theme. The whole sentence runs: "War is the father of all good things; war is also the father of good prose." Chen Quan quoted only the first half—the Heraclitean half, not the Nietzschean half, thus making Nietzsche sound a warmonger.[14] The third passage, "The poison of which weaker natures perish strengthens the strong—nor do they call it poison," was originally meant to express the idea that adverse external and internal conditions could turn out to be "favorable" to the formation of great characters.[15] Chen Quan quoted it out of context and thereby giving it a sinister overtone.

Through misunderstanding, mistranslating, and arbitrary editing, Chen Quan created a Nietzsche that was shamelessly immoral and philosophically unintelligent. He then glorified his own creation. Academic incompetence alone cannot account for such a phenomenon. A better explanation has to be sought in Chen Quan's intellectual background.

Eight year before his "From Schopenhauer to Nietzsche," Chen Quan published a philosophical novel *Questioning the Heaven* (1928). The novel's hero, Lin Yunzhang, thirsted for power even when he was only a child. In his teen years, he went to work as an apprentice in a drugstore where he fell in love with the shop keeper's daughter. Due to his humble origin, he could not hope to win the girl's heart. He then joined a warlord's army and was promoted to a senior position. In endless wars among warlords, Lin Yunzhang was transformed into "a heartless devil who kills without the slightest remorse. "[16] As the story goes, he was sent to govern his hometown, where he found his sweetheart already a married woman. He pretended to be a friend to her family at first, and then had the husband murdered and married the widow.

A remarkable feature of the novel is the complete moral depravity of its characters. In Chen Quan's fictional world, not a single person displays a trace of noble sentiment. Almost everyone betrays someone else at his first convenience. There are only two exceptions: one figure in the novel is killed treacherously before he had a chance to betray others; the other, mentally retarded, does not know how to betray. Through the mouth of Lin Yunzhang, Chen Quan commented: "The world is cruel and ruthless. If you do not kill others, others will kill you."[17]

This world created by Chen Quan is a typical "cannibalistic society," if we borrow Lu Xun's rhetoric. The question Chen Quan intended to raise in his *Questioning the Heaven*, however, is not how to overturn the "banquet of human flesh," as in the case of Lu Xun and other left-wing writers. His fictional hero entered the "banquet" with a good appetite but was constantly disappointed at what he got. After killing numerous people, Lin Yunzhang returned to his hometown with power and money only to find his beloved girl already married. He murdered her husband and married her only to be disappointed in her. Besides, the very power and money he had acquired were eventually lost due to the vicissitude of wars. The novel ends with Lin Yunzhang lying sick and completely disillusioned.

The article "From Schopenhauer to Nietzsche" can be best understood if seen as a sequence to his early novel. When Chen Quan talked about Schopenhauer's pessimism, criticizing him for "negating life," he actually had the disillusioned Lin Yunzhang in mind. He found a cure for Lin Yunzhang in what he considered to be Nietzsche's "life-affirming" philosophy, that is, cannibalism-affirming philosophy. Chen Quan quoted Nietzsche as saying: "The only happiness resides in work: All of you ought to work together and enjoy happiness in every one of your acts."[18] For Lin Yunzhang and other willing guests of the "banquet of human flesh," the message is clear: Don't be disheartened if you are not fully satisfied with your meals, just enjoy preparing such banquets.

Chen Quan's next writing on Nietzsche was a politically motivated one. In a journal published in the fall of 1937, his essay "Nietzsche and Modern Historical Education" appeared immediately after another essay about history, "Idealism in Historical Science and its Critique," written by Jian Bozen, a Marxist historian.[19] The coexistence of a Nietzschean essay and a Marxist essays had been made possible by the United Front recently formed in response to Japan's full scale invasion. These essays were not mere academic discussions, but part of an ongoing ideological debate within the United Front between the Nationalists and the Communists.

Jian Bozan seems to be influenced by one of Plekhanov's pamphlets about the individual's role in history. He first gave an overview of historical materialism and then criticized a variety of "idealist" views of history. Invoking Lenin's theory of imperialism, he characterized the rise of Fascism as a necessary consequence of capitalism. Jian Bozan discussed three issues: history is not created by a few "great men" or "leaders," but by the masses; the bourgeois society is to be replaced by a better social system as a historical necessity; and the course of history is not determined by violence. Jian Bozan's essay can be read as an endorsement of the CCP's view that China should mobilize the masses in its war against Japan, instead of relying only on the military and Generalissimo Chiang Kai-shek.

Chen Quan's essay "Nietzsche and Modern Historical Education" was based on a paraphrase of "On the Advantage and Disadvantage of History for Life" from *Untimely Meditations*. Chen Quan intended to use Nietzsche to counter the influence of Marx and to support the GMD's war policy. Just as his earlier article, it is full of distortions and errors. For example, it presents Nietzsche as rejecting the universal relevance of history:

> History can be useful only to the minority, not to the majority; only to adults,

not to youth; only to great men, not to mediocre men. The former can manipulate history, the latter are manipulated by history.[20]

Nietzsche had never held such a view. In "On the Advantage and Disadvantage of History for Life," Nietzsche demonstrated how history, in its various forms, could serve life. He believed that "every man and every nation" requires "a certain knowledge of the past."[21] What he considered harmful to youth is not history itself but an excess of historical sense, more specifically, the kind of bourgeois historicism that dominated German historical science and education.

Chen Quan also asserted that Nietzsche advocated "forgetfulness" because history is dangerous:

> If a man feels historicity in everything, he would be like a man who dares not sleep, or an animal that dares not stop eating and drinking. Therefore a happy life is possible only when there is no memory. Actually life is impossible without forgetfulness. To a certain degree, the concept of history is like sleeplessness: it can destroy a man, a nation or a culture.[22]

These are not Nietzsche's views at all. Nietzsche assumed that only animals live in complete forgetfulness and he considered history to be harmful only under certain conditions:

> *There is a degree of sleeplessness, of rumination, of historical sense, which is harmful and ultimately fatal to the living thing, whether it be a man, a people or a culture.* To determine this degree, and therewith the boundary at which the past has to be forgotten if it is not to become the gravedigger of the present, one would have to know exactly how great the *plastic power* of a man, a people, a culture is.... The stronger the innermost roots of a man's nature, the more readily will he be able to assimilate and appropriate the things of the past; and the most powerful and tremendous nature would be characterized by the fact that it would know no boundary at all at which the historical sense began to overwhelm it; it would draw to itself and incorporate into itself all the past, its own and that most foreign to it, and as it were transform it into blood.... *the unhistorical and the historical are necessary in equal measure for the health of an individual, of a people and of a culture.*[23]

In the final section of his essay, Chen Quan asserted that Nietzsche expected youth to use the "unhistorical" and the "suprahistorical" to resist science.[24] He also told his readers that Nietzsche praised the ancient Greeks for liberating themselves "from the past and from the invading foreign cultures, forming their own culture through fierce wars."[25] The political implications were obvious here, for Marxists had claimed to have truly understood history and Marxism had been attacked in China on the ground of its foreign origin. On these two issues, however, Nietzsche was not on Chen Quan's side. Chen Quan did not tell his readers that, in "On the Advantage and Disadvantage of History for Life," Nietzsche also asked youth to be "sufficiently healthy again to study history."[26] Far from being a xenophobe, Nietzsche praised the Greeks for their ability to "gradually organize the chaos" of many foreign cultures and he called the Greeks "the happiest enrichers and augmenters of the treasure they had inherited." Nietzsche did not talk about "fierce wars" against foreign cultures. What he said was that the Greeks had gone through "hard struggles with themselves" before they were able to creatively appropriate foreign cultures according to their own needs.[27]

If his essay was full of distortions, Chen Quan was not mistaken on one point—the difference between Nietzsche and Marx in their social values. He paraphrased Nietzsche's criticism of Eduard von Hartmann (1842-1906), highlighting Nietzsche's contempt for the latter's vision of "a future stage of social evolution at which every worker, "having a workday which leaves him adequate leisure for intellectual training, leads a comfortable existence." Based on this Chen Quan maintained that "a truly ideal society" could only be built by "great individuals," not by the "ignorant masses."[28]

The covered ideological clash between the left and the right in a journal had probably drawn little public attention at a time when fierce battles between Japanese and Chinese troops were raging in northern and central China. But the positions taken by the two sides foreshadowed the outcome of the future contest for power between the Communists and the Nationalists. In the debate the Chinese right had yielded the ground of science to their Marxist opponents and thus making themselves look absurd and obsolete. Moreover, their pseudo-Nietzschean contempt for the masses could only alienate themselves from the Chinese population. The debate between Chen Quan and Jian Bozan exemplifies how the GMD had lost the ideological battle to the CCP long before they were defeated militarily.

Three years after writing "Nietzsche and Modern Historical Education," Chen Quan became the central figure of a pro-Fascist movement in China. In April 1940, as if responding to the German offensive across the French border, the journal *Strategies of the Warring States* was launched in Kunming, a city that sheltered some of China's best universities during the war.[29] Its founders and contributors formed a semi-academic and semi-political circle, generally referred to as the "The Strategies of the Warring States Group [Hereafter referred to as the "Strategies Group"]." When the journal stopped publication in the summer of 1941, the "Strategies Group" created "Warring States," a weekly feature page in a newspaper, as their new forum.[30]

In the first issue of *Strategies of the Warring States*, Lin Tongji, one of its founders, wrote an editorial, "The Return of the Epoch of the Warring States." According to Lin Tongji, history evolves in an expanding cyclical movement. Two thousand years ago, China had passed from the "epoch of the Warring States" to that of a unified empire. A similar transition was occurring on a global scale now. The world was moving from the stage of "Warring States" to that of a unified world state. These ideas were not Lin Tongji's invention but were plagiarized by him from Oswald Spengler's *Decline of the West*.[31] Based on this Spenglerian analogy, Lin Tongji proposed that China accommodate itself to the world process and create a "totalitarian state," with Germany, Italy and the Soviet Union as its models.[32]

If China's pro-Fascist movement received its name from Oswald Spengler, it's soul was Friedrich Nietzsche. Chen Quan, the journal's co-founder, became the mot active theorist of the "Strategies Group." On June 25, 1940, three days after Germany forced France to sign an armistice, Chen Quan's essay "The Character and Ideas of the German Nation" appeared in *Strategies of Warring States*. He asked his readers not to see Hitler as an isolated phenomenon but as representing "the characters and ideals of the German nation." He referred to Nietzsche as "the most pronounced anti-democratic thinker" who, along with Fichte and Hegel, held such views as that individuals must subordinate themselves to the state; that the leader is the locus of the national spirit; and that the masses must worship the leader and die for him. He warned that, given the victorious march of the Nazis, no other nation could survive if they did not adopt "a new attitude, a new approach, and a new spirit."[33]

In order to promote these German "characters and ideals" in China, Chen Quan wrote a dozen or so essays, of which five were about Nietzsche: "The Thought of Nietzsche" [尼采的思想]; "the Political Thought of Nietzsche" [尼采的政治思想]; "Nietzsche and Women" [尼采與女性]; "Nietzsche's Moral Ideas" [尼采的道德觀念]; "Nietzsche's Atheism" [尼采的無神論]). Although most ideas expressed in these essays were not new to him, they were far more blatantly spelled out now. Chen Quan was no longer concerned with academic format and he simply made one assertion about Nietzsche after another. For example, he told his readers that

Nietzsche disliked modern states because they protected the masses and stifled supermen. He contemplated, "If there will be a new state organization in which superman assumes dictatorial power, then that state symbolizes the 'will to power' and Nietzsche would have no reason not to accept it." Under the "superman dictatorship," supermen and geniuses would have the "absolute freedom to develop themselves":

> In such a society, the strong ought to conquer the weak, the wise ought to dominate the unwise. We should have no sympathy at all for the weak and the unwise, because they have no right to live in the world at all. The territories they have occupied should be reserved for a superior people.[34]

Such views naturally drew fire from both the liberals and the Marxists. In response, Chen Quan accused his critics of "weakening the spirit of national solidarity, promoting a psychology of national dependency [referring to Western allies and the Soviet Union], delaying political unification, and diverting military resources." He called for "a powerful government capable of making thorough plans in regard to military affairs, politics, economy, and education."[35]

Chen Quan wrote a number of short stories and plays in the early 1940s. Some of these appear to illustrate his Nietzschean ideas. One of his stories is about an "Auntie Wang," who was the illegitimate daughter of a ragpicker and was brought up in an orphanage. "Auntie Wang" had never learned to read or write and she knew nothing about politics. Yet, influenced by Comrade Xu, a communist activist, she joined a demonstration against the government. The police dispersed the demonstration and arrested Comrade Xu, who turned out to be a lunatic escaped from an asylum. Through such a story Chen Quan apparently intended to show his Nietzschean contempt for the mass movement.[36]

Wild Rose, one of Chen Quan's better known war time plays, is a melodrama about an undercover operation behind the enemy line. The struggle between the Japanese occupation and the resistance is portrayed as a competition in treachery, ruthlessness and cruelty. Eventually the chief villain, Wang Limin, a collaborator, is outmaneuvered by a number of GMD secret agents planted around him, including his wife, a trusted servant, and a close friend. *The Golden Ring*, another play by Chen Quan, tells the story of a bandit chief who put his force under Japanese command, in order to receive military equipment from the Japanese and then defect to the Nationalist government. Such plays are similar to his early novel *Questioning the Heaven* in one respect: they describe a world in which everyone betrays someone else. There is only one difference: now the betrayal is done in the name of the nation and the Generalissimo and is therefore justified and affirmed.[37] These plays also show how Chen Quan understood the idea of "life-affirming."

The Chinese right's flirtation with the Nazis did not last long. In June 1942 the Allied victory in the Far East was assured after the US navy had dealt a fatal blow to the Japanese navy in the Battle of Midway. The next month, the weekly feature page "Warring States" was dumped by its host newspaper. With it, the "Strategies Group" dissolved into its elements. Hereafter Chen Quan stopped talking about Nietzsche and began to advocate a "nationalistic" literature. Thus ended this infamous episode in the Chinese reception of Nietzsche.

Notes

[1] Chen Quan, "The Coup" and "Dismissal," in *Blue Butterflies* (Shanghai: Commercial Press, 1940), 105-116.

[2] Nietzsche, "Attempt at a Self-Criticism," in *Basic Writings*, trans. Walter Kaufmann (New York: Random House, 1968), 24.

[3] Chen Quan, "From Schopenhauer to Nietzsche," *Tsinghuan Journal* vol. 11, no. 2 (April, 1936): 489.

[4] Nietzsche, "The Birth of Tragedy," *Basic Writings*, 36-37.

[5] Chen Quan, 1936: 478.

[6] Nietzsche, *Basic Writings*, 35-36.

[7] Chen Quan, 1936: 481-482.

[8] Nietzsche, *Untimely Meditations*, tran. R. J. Hollingdale (Cambridge: Cambridge Universtiy Press, 1983), 153-154.

[9] Chen Quan, 1936: 513, 488-489, 492.

[10] Nietzsche, *Human, All Too Human: A Book for Free Spirit*, trans. R. J. Hollingdale (Cambridge and New York: Cambridge University Press, 1986), 119.

[11] *Ibid.*, 50, 323.

[12] Nietzsche, *The Gay Science*, trans. Walter Kaufmann (New York: Vintage Books, 1974), 100.

[13] Chen Quan, 1936: 502.

[14] Chen Quan, 1936: 502; Nietzsche, *The Gay Science*, 145.

[15] Chen, 1936: 502; Nietzsche, *The Gay Science*, 91-92.

[16] Chen Quan, *Questioning the Heaven* (Jiangsu Wenyi Press, 1985), 137. The book was originally published in 1928.

[17] *Ibid.*, 207.
[18] Chen Quan, 1936: 507. Source unclear.
[19] Chen Quan, "Nietzsche and Modern Historical Education," [尼采與近代曆史教育] and Jian Bozan, "Idealism in Historical Science and its Critique," in *Quarterly of the Sun Yet-sen Institute of Culture and Education* [中山文化教育館季刊], Fall 1937.
[20] *Ibid.*, 1177.
[21] Nietzsche, *Untimely*, 77.
[22] *Quarterly*, 1179.
[23] Nietzsche, *Untimely*, 62-63.
[24] *Quarterly*, 1192.
[25] *Ibid.*.
[26] Nietzsche, *Untimely*, 122.
[27] Nietzsche, *Untimely*, 122-123.
[28] Nietzsche, *Untimely*, 108-121; and *Quarterly*, 1190.
[29] The journal *Strategies of Warring States* [戰國策] was first published on April 15, 1940.
[30] The weekly feature page [《大公報》" 戰國 " 副刊] started on December 3, 1941 in Chongqing, the provisional capital of China. It stopped publication on July 1 of the next year.
[31] See Oswald Spengler, *Der Untergang Des Abendlandes, Zweiter Band: Welthistorische Perspecktiven* [The Decline of the West, Vol. 2: Perspectives of World History] (München: C. H. Beck'sche Werlagsbuchhandlung, 1922), 521-540.
[32] Su Guangwen, *Selected Sources of Literary Theories* (Chengdu: Sichuan Education Press, 1988), 301-312.
[33] Beijing Normal University, Dept. of Chinese Literature, *Sources of Contemporary Literature* [北京師範大學中文系,《中國現代文學史參考資料》] (Beijing, Beijing Normal Univerity Press, 1959): Vol. 1, Part 2, 717-718 and Su Guangwen, 321.
[34] Chen Quan, "Nietzsche's Political Thought," [尼采的政治思想] *Warring States* no. 9 (August 1940): 21-24.
[35] Chen Quan, "Political Ideals and the Ideal Politics," *Da Gong Bao*, January 28, 1942, the weekly feature page "Warring States." From Jia Zhifang, *Literary Associations and Schools of Contemporary China* [南京:江蘇教育出版社,《中國現代文學社團流派》] (Nanjing: Jiansu Education Press, 1989), 750-751.
[36] Chen Quan, "Auntie Wang's Political Involvement," in Chen Quan, *Blue Butterflies*, 38-46.
[37] Chen Quan, *Wild Rose* [野玫瑰] (Chongqing: Commercial Press, 1942). Originally published in *Journal of Humanities*, [《文史雜誌》] vol. 1, no. 6-8 (June 16 to July 17, 1941.); and *The Golden Ring* [金指環] in *Military Affairs and Politics*, [《軍事與政治》] vol. 2, no. 5 and no. 6, vol. 3. no. 1, published from April to June, 1942.

CHAPTER 8

Zhou Guoping:

Nietzsche At the Turn of the Century

Nietzsche was no longer a figure of public attention after the "Strategies Group" episode. In fact, all intellectual activities were much overshadowed by the war with Japan (1937-1945) and the civil war between the Nationalists and the Communists (1946-1949). Nietzsche, however, continued to enjoy a sizable readership in China, as evidenced by the reprinting of older translations of Nietzsche and the publication of a new and better translation of *Thus Spoke Zarathustra* by Chu Tunan.[1]

The three decades between 1949 and 1978 were a period of critical importance in regard to the Chinese reception of Western philosophy. The CCP leaders' overzealous efforts to promote Marxism as state orthodoxy had left a complex legacy. In a period when individuals were being punished for holding views different from the official ideology, free inquiry of philosophical issues had become all but impossible. What was left for scholars to do was to "criticize" non-Marxist thinkers, all deemed deficient in one way or another, if not outright reactionary. Nietzsche was a taboo of taboos. He, according to the official catechism, was the spokesman of imperialism, fascism and nazism, therefore one of the worst "bourgeois" philosophers that ever existed in history. Consequently Nietzsche had vanished from the intellectual stage in the Chinese mainland.* With the

---

* Since 1949, the mainland and Taiwan have followed different lines of development, politically and culturally. I have to leave the subject of Nietzsche's influence in Taiwan to better qualified historians.

exception of a reprint of *Thus spoke Zarathustra* in 1952, no books by Nietzsche or about Nietzsche were published during this period. In libraries across China, Nietzsche's works were withdrawn from general circulation and put in "restricted shelves," accessible only to officials in charge of propaganda, who occasionally needed a whipping boy in their campaigns against bourgeois ideas.

However, one should not view the People's Republic of China in its first three decades merely as an intellectual desert. The harmful effects of thought control and censorship in the Mao Zedong era had been partly offset by some positive developments. One of such developments was the rise of a whole generation of intellectuals who, though not necessarily Marxists, were well trained in Marxist theory. The CCP's efforts to promote Marxism had persuaded or forced many intellectuals to read volumes of Marxist classics that they would never have read otherwise. In order to better understand Marxism, they sought out the works of Hegel, Feuerbach, French "Utopian socialists," and other Western thinkers. In the process many had acquired a genuine interest in Marxism and in Western philosophy in general. Besides, many of them were not ignorant of more recent philosophical developments in the West. Through the Philosophy and Social Science Section of the Chinese Academy of Sciences,* the CCP had authorized the translation of many modern and contemporary Western works (Nietzsche not included), with the belief that Marxists should engage in fighting "bourgeois ideas." Although such publications were earmarked for "restricted circulation," which meant for party propaganda officers, they actually reached a much wider circle through various channels. Thus in the Mao Zedong era a generation of intellectuals grew up with a sound knowledge of Marxist classics and some knowledge of Western philosophical tradition in general. Although handicapped by the scarcity of books and by intellectual isolation, they were professionals so far as Marxist theory was concerned and were well prepared to explore other Western theories. In contrast, most pre-1949 intellectuals were dilettantes in philosophy. For instance, none of the figures discussed so far in the current book had been willing or capable to follow through a systematic study of Nietzsche's works, if they had read him at all.

---

* The Philosophy and Social Science Section of the Chinese Academy of Sciences [中國科學院哲學社會科學部, 簡稱學部] was the predecessor of the Chinese Academy of Social Sciences.

The state's sponsorship of Marxist studies had another unexpected effect: it had torn down a most formidable barrier to Chinese assimilation of Western ideas—the barrier of language. For over two millennia the Chinese had been using classical Chinese in writing on most occasions. It was in the beginning of the 20th century, especially during the New Culture Movement, that some Chinese intellectuals began to experiment with writing in vernacular Chinese, a writing style that has since evolved into modern Chinese. By necessity modern Chinese was limited in vocabulary and syntax in the beginning and it had remained a language with many uncertainties for a long time. No standard vocabulary existed for Western philosophical concepts. When discussing Western philosophy, a Chinese writer had to improvise his own terminology by one of the following means: to use Chinese words with identical or similar meanings, to create words by new combinations of single Chinese characters, to borrow from Japanese, to transcribe the sounds of the original words, or to simply use the original words without translation. Such an anarchy of usage made meaningful philosophical discourses all but impossible. Moreover, the syntax of modern Chinese in its early stage was too simple: the sentences were short and loosely organized, with few grammatical devices to indicate the relationships between sentence components. When translating Western philosophical works, a Chinese writer had to break up long sentences and turn them into short and choppy ones, resulting in inaccurate, unnatural and often incomprehensible texts. Although modern Chinese made significant headway in the three decades following the New Culture Movement, by 1949 it had remained an awkward vehicle for foreign philosophical ideas.

After 1949, in their effort to promote the study of Marxism, Mao Zedong and other leaders of the People's Republic of China engineered a major scholarly project—the translation of all Marxist classics, including revising some existent translations. The government recruited China's best experts in Western language and philosophy to the Bureau for the Compilation and Translation of the Works of Marx, Engels, Lenin and Stalin, an organization directly supervised by the CCP's Central Committee [中共中央馬恩列斯著作編譯局]. In a country where Marxism was supposed to guide all activities, the work of translating Marxist classics was not a casual exertion. In order to achieve accuracy and beauty, the translators meticulously examined every sentence, carefully weighed possible variations of vocabulary and syntax, strictly maintained consistency in the use of vocabulary, extensively annotated philosophical terms and proper names. The painstaking efforts of the Bureau's experts left a monument of the Mao Zedong era, the multi-volume Chinese version of the *Complete Works of Marx and Engels*.[2] In the process these Chinese Martin Luthers had created more sophisticated syntax and established standard vocabulary for ideas of Western origin, thus making it a mature language, capable of conveying complicated ideas with precision and grace.

In the era of Deng Xiaoping, when China's new leadership had gotten rid of the worst form of censorship and ideological control and adopted a more liberal policy, the pent-up energy of a generation of intellectuals trained in Marxism and versed in mature modern Chinese was suddenly released, giving rise to the unprecedented flourishing of scholarship in Western philosophy in the 1980s and 1990s. Nietzsche's fortune was gradually reversed. After a ban of nearly thirty years, works by and about Nietzsche were published again. In the first few years, some party officers still felt obliged to warn the public against Nietzsche's malignant influence.[3] But some writers began to question the stereotype of Nietzsche as a reactionary philosopher by pointing to his influence over Lu Xun and other prominent writers on the left.[4]

The rehabilitation of Nietzsche gathered full momentum in 1985 when Ru Xin, vice chairman of the Chinese Academy of Social Sciences, wrote an essay on Nietzsche. Instead of treating him as a prophet of fascism, Ru Xin categorized Nietzsche as belonging to "that part of the bourgeoisie and petty bourgeoisie which were disillusioned with the status quo in Germany but unable to find a way out." Through analyzing *The Birth of Tragedy*, he argued that "so far as tragedy leads people to a positive and active attitude toward life, Nietzsche is much closer to Hegel." He compared the Dionysian to "a Faustian spirit in a distorted form."[5] As one of the leading Marxist theorists in China, Ru Xin's benevolent criticism broke the taboo about Nietzsche. Soon other writers began to talk about how Nietzsche's works had been falsified by his sister and distorted by the Nazis and how Nietzsche detested narrow-minded nationalism and anti-Semitism.[6] Toward the end of 1985, George Brandes's *Nietzsche*, translated by An Yanming, was published and became a bestseller.[7]

Since then a "Nietzsche fever" had developed in China, especially among the young. The amount of works by and about Nietzsche published over the few years after 1985 exceeded all that had been published in the previous eight decades combined. Most new translations are of good quality, testifying to the maturation of modern Chinese. Critical works produced in the same period, on the other hand, are quite uneven in quality. Not a few writers merely repeated erroneous views about Nietzsche that were circulating in the 1920s and 1930s. Some others had invented new ways of distorting and vulgarizing Nietzsche. However, the best scholars in China had brought the overall standard of Nietzsche scholarship to a much higher level, almost a miracle considering the fact that Nietzsche had been a taboo for over three decades. Zhou Guoping, a graduate student and researcher in the Chinese Academy of Social Sciences, emerged as China's leading scholar on Nietzsche. His well-informed interpretation and his accurate and graceful translation sets him far apart from any figure discussed so far in the current book.

Zhou Guoping belongs to the generation of Chinese intellectuals that was trained in the Marxist tradition in the Mao Zedong era. In 1949 when the People's Republic of China was founded he was only four years old. Fourteen years later, in 1963, he was admitted to the Department of Philosophy at Beijing University, where, beside studying Marxist classics, he read Descartes and Hume with great interest and enjoyed many Western literary works.[8] In 1968, during the Cultural Revolution, he was sent to the Guangxi province, first working in a propaganda department and, a few years later, in a party academy. When the Chinese Academy of Social Sciences was founded in Beijing in 1978 Zhou Guoping enrolled in its graduate school where he was to receive both his M.S. degree and Ph.D. degree. Since 1981 he has been a researcher the academy's Institute of Philosophy.

In the early years of the reform era, many Chinese intellectuals were more interested in Marxism than in any other philosophical school. They were attracted to new interpretations of Marxism by scholars from the Soviet Union and other East European Countries, by representatives of Eurocommunism and the New Left in the West. Through elaborating on Marx's theory of alienation and treating Marxism as part of Western humanist tradition, they initiated what can be called a New Marxist Movement. The movement reached a climax in 1983 at the one hundredth anniversary of Marx's death when Zhou Yang and other leading Marxist intellectuals launched a concerted attack on undemocratic aspects of China's political system. The New Marxist Movement brought a sharp backlash. Some Marxist fundamentalists within the CCP initiated a counterattack, not only accusing the New Marxist Movement as "spiritual pollution," but also trying to roll back the party's reform policy. The CCP leadership, in order to focus on its project of economic reforms, soon put the ideological warfare within the party to an end.

Zhou Guoping had studied Marxism as a humanist tradition in the early 1980s. After realizing that Marxism, as the official ideology, was a field too sensitive politically and therefore untouchable, he turned to study Nietzsche.[9] Between 1985 and 1989, by discussing key issues of Nietzsche's philosophy in articles and books and by translating *The Birth of Tragedy: Selected Aesthetic Works of Nietzsche*, *The Twilight of Idols* and some other works by Nietzsche, he contributed more than anyone else to the understanding of Nietzsche in China in the period.

Zhou Guoping's booklet *Nietzsche at the Turn of the Century*, published in July 1986, was the most popular writing on Nietzsche at the time. While covering all major aspects of Nietzsche's philosophy, the booklet was not a balanced introduction. In its preface, Zhou Guoping explained that he was presenting the more positive aspects of Nietzsche's philosophy in order to "correct a bias" against the German philosopher that had prevailed in China for many years.[10] Later he acknowledged that studying Nietzsche "did nothing more than supply... a convenient scholarly expression" of his own thought.[11] A question naturally arises: if he was trying to express his own views through Nietzsche, did he maintain his intellectual integrity as an interpreter? Zhou Guoping himself was aware of the risk involved. He once quoted Lu Xiangshan, a Chinese philosopher of the 12th century, who characterized his attitude toward ancient classics as "I annotate the Six Classics and the Six Classics also annotate me." Zhou Guoping explained his own position:

> After all, scholarly studies are different from literary creation, there have to be some restrictions on imagination. Even if it is a matter of "annotating one's own ideas with the Six Classics," one still has to know the Six Classics well and to offer convincing proofs.[12]

Zhou Guoping was indeed very familiar with Nietzsche's works as he demonstrated in *Nietzsche at the Turn of the Century*. To better elucidate Nietzsche's ideas, he quoted extensively from him, often in accurate and elegant modern Chinese. Although on rare occasions he twisted Nietzsche to make his own point, his interpretation was largely based on Nietzsche's own words.

Zhou Guoping did not claim the booklet to be a scholarly work, but described it as "at best a collection of notes and reflections on Nietzsche's works."[13] By any standard *Nietzsche at the Turn of the Century* is a highly organized book. The first chapter examines the relation between Nietzsche and many philosophic trends in the twentieth century. The second chapter, "In Front of the Canvas of Life" could well have been renamed "Nietzsche as a Philosopher." Both in style and content, it is modeled on Nietzsche's "Schopenhauer as an Educator." The chapter ends with a comparison of Marx and Nietzsche. The former is said to stand for a "macro-sociology" that studies man as a social and historical being while the latter a "micro-psychology" that reveals the irrational existence of man as an individual.[14] From Chapters three to eight, each chapter studies a few Nietzschean concepts, grouped according to their inner logic.

The first group includes the Dionysian, the will to power, and the eternal recurrence. According to the author, any philosophy has to search for a unity between the individual and the totality. In the case of Nietzsche, the totality is the universe's eternal becoming. The Dionysian, the will to power and the eternal recurrence are but three manifestations of this same totality. Nietzsche, in *The Birth of Tragedy*, inherited Schopenhauer's view about the will to life as the ultimate reality and carried it to its logical conclusion. If the will to life is the essence of existence, then it has to be eternal by its very nature, it has to constantly destroy and create individual life. Zhou Guoping explains:

> Nietzsche gave meaning to individual existence through the concept of the universal life. He demanded that individuals, from the standpoint of the universal life, welcome the eternal becoming, including the destruction of finite individuals.[15]

An individual can accept such a viewpoint only through "the Dionysian," a mystic status of existence where an individual is united with the universal will to life.

When discussing the concept of the "will to power" Zhou Guoping has abandoned the established Chinese translation of the phrase [權力意志], which suggests political power more than anything else, in favor of a new translation [強力意志] that points to power in general. In his opinion, Nietzsche, by substituting the "will to power" for the "will to life," set himself apart from both Darwin and Schopenhauer. Life, in its totality, is characterized by "abundance, profusion, even absurd squandering." The issue, therefore, is not that of the Darwinian "struggle for survival" but of the Nietzschean "expansion of power".[16] The will to power also corrects Schopenhauer's view about life and will. Life is something that must constantly transcend itself and overcome its limitations. "Yeasayers to life" do not merely preserve their life, but increase their power and vitality through creative activities.

What Zhou Guoping thought problematic about the will to power is not the theory itself but the conclusion Nietzsche drew from it. Nietzsche viewed the will to power as unevenly distributed among people and therefore supported an elite minority's right to rule over others. Zhou Guoping called such ideas as the "dregs of Nietzsche's philosophy."[17]

Zhou Guoping maintained that Nietzsche was always a pessimist at heart for he was unable to recover from a "wound" he had received from Schopenhauer's metaphysics. Nietzsche created the theory of the eternal recurrence in order to bring about the union of man and eternity. But this theory turned out to be more of a nightmare than a consolation. Only through *"amor fati,"* was Nietzsche able to reconcile the idea of the eternal recurrence with the Dionysian and the will to power:

> When Nietzsche stressed that the highest degree of affirmation is possible only when the eternal recurrence is accepted as fate, he was actually saying that life is meaningless, and the Yeasayers should accept this meaningless life as it is. After seeing through the true nature of life—the meaninglessness of life, if you still love life and glorify it, only then you prove yourself a true tragic hero, and only then you arrive at the ultimate affirmation of life. There is a heroism in this attitude, but unmistakably there is also a desperation in it.[18]

By treating "the Dionysian," "the will to power," and "the eternal recurrence" as originating from the same yearning for a transcendental meaning in a universe without God, Zhou Guoping has brought the discussion of Nietzsche's philosophy to a realm not reached by earlier Chinese writers.*

The next chapter is about human nature and the concept of freedom. Zhou Guoping pointed to the fact that many contemporary philosophic schools, including Western Marxist philosophy, emphasize man's incompleteness, openness and infinite potential. Nietzsche's view of human nature is built upon the same "modern premise." Since man is not a pre-defined animal, and has an infinite potential to develop along different lines, man's valuation becomes the determining factor of freedom. Nietzsche, Zhou Guoping explains, recognized the dialectics of human valuation. Valuation imparts meaning to life. It gives a purpose to life that is higher

---

* He included a more elaborate analysis of "the eternal recurrence" in his other book, see p. 130.

than life itself. Man's undefined nature and his persistent seeking for meaning have enabled him to rise above other animals. However, while man's valuation is indispensable from an anthropocentric point of view, the values thus created are nothing but "lies" or "misunderstandings" when judged against the "truth" of nature and the universe. From a certain point in history onward, these values created by man begin to threaten himself. They diminish man's vitality, destroy his healthy instincts and threaten to return him to the status of a well-defined animal. Zhou Guoping explained Nietzsche's solution:

> Among many choices that are open to him, man ought to choose those that will guarantee his access to further choices. That is, man should always remain undefined, man's every activity of self-creation should simultaneously create freedom for new creation. Therefore Nietzsche has proposed a new kind of morality for creators.[19]

Zhou Guoping made an attempt to solve a seeming contradiction between Nietzsche's refutation of "freedom of will" and his highly voluntarist view of the will. He speculated that Nietzsche refuted the freedom of will only to absolve man from his responsibility to any transcendental moral purpose and thereby encourage him to be free and creative. "Becoming is innocent. Men neither have any transcendental sin nor any responsibility to repent." "Once outside the realm of morality, once the individual will truly apprehends the truth of the becoming and change of the universal will, it acquires freedom. This is the will to create."[20]

Zhou Guoping treated Nietzsche's three metamorphoses of the spirit as three defining qualities of freedom. The camel represents the acquisition of power through self-overcoming and overcoming resistance. The lion represents valuation, the independence of the will from all existing values. The child represents creation, by which the individual will participates in becoming and achieves a union with the universal will.

Chapter five discusses the concept of self. Zhou Guoping maintained that what Nietzsche referred to as the true "self" has two layers. The bottom layer refers to man's instinct, various unconscious cravings, emotions, feelings and experiences; the upper layer refers to a spiritual "self," product of one's self creation. Although the bottom layer is the source of energy and the foundation for the upper layer, the upper layer is the more important one. Zhou Guoping eloquently demonstrated how Nietzsche's "healthy selfishness" is different from the bourgeoisie's profit seeking and from the Christian love. Zhou Guoping did not agree with Nietzsche on every point.

He found in Nietzsche a tendency to view individuals as inherently in antagonistic relationships and to ignore the fact that "society is the only locus for self-realization and individual development." Besides, thought Zhou Guoping, there is an inconsistency in Nietzsche's concept of "healthy selfishness." Theoretically all individuals should be able to develop unique and good characters on the basis of "healthy selfishness." But Nietzsche allowed most people to serve as tools for a minority. The chapter concludes with the following comment:

> Nietzsche was dissatisfied with the status quo of the bourgeois society. Instead of formulating a more progressive social ideal, he was always nostalgic of a hierarchical society based largely on slavery. This is a most distressing contradiction in Nietzsche's thought.[21]

The next chapter introduces Nietzsche's criticism of reason, science, rationalism, and language. In Zhou Guoping's view, while having recognized the limitations of rationality, Nietzsche did not advocate irrationality. To elaborate on Nietzsche's statement that "Flesh is big reason, spirit is small reason that serves the flesh" (*Thus spoke Zarathustra*), Zhou Guoping quoted the following passage from *The Gay Science*:

> Whether I contemplate men with benevolence or with an evil eye, I always find them concerned with a single task, all of them and every one of them in particular: to do what is good for the preservation of the human race.... the instinct for preservation of the species—erupts as reason and as passion of the spirit.[22]

He then drew his conclusion:

> We must understand that when Nietzsche emphasized the instincts of life he had the species in mind; when such instincts are expressed in an individual, they are the individual's inner vitality.[23]

Indeed there is nothing irrational in the idea that reason or science should be subordinated to the interest of the "species." But the idea did not come from Nietzsche. When quoting from *The Gay Science*, Zhou Guoping had intentionally left out the following words:

> Hatred, the mischievous delight in the misfortunes of others, the lust to rob and dominate, and whatever else is called evil belongs to the most amazing economy of the preservation of the species.[24]

Purged of its irrational element, the concept of the "species" is no longer that of Nietzsche but identical to young Marx's "species being" (from

Economic and Philosophical Manuscripts of 1844). This is one of the few instances when Zhou Guoping promoted Marxist ideas through reinterpreting Nietzsche.

The seventh chapter—"revaluation of all values"—explains why Nietzsche criticized Christian morality and what Nietzsche meant by life-affirming. Zhou Guoping summed up the idea of revaluation as "first seeing through the irrelevance of good and evil from the viewpoint of nature, life and becoming, then constructing a new valuation of good and evil from the viewpoint of nature, life and becoming."[25] Such an attitude is said to be the opposite of Christian morality:

> The issue is: "How can one spiritualize, beautify, deify a craving?" that is how to sublimate a craving. But Christian morality has never asked this question, its practice and its 'cure' is castration.... It has at all times emphasized discipline by extirpation. But an attack on the roots of passion means an attack on the roots of life." Its only capability is to be hostile to life.[26]

The quoted words are from section 76 of *Twilight of the Idols*. But they are not Nietzsche's original words. Zhou Guoping had edited Nietzsche's text, not to save space—the original text is even shorter—but to avoid an inconvenience. In the original text, Nietzsche was more specific in regard to "extirpation"—it was the "extirpation (of sensuality, of pride, of the lust to rule, of avarice, of vengefulness)."[27] In contrast, Zhou Guoping, in this booklet and his other writings, dodged the issue of man's antisocial and destructive instincts. For him man's instincts appear to be quite innocent, comprising only sexual desire and its sublimated derivatives.

The omission of the negative set of man's instincts must be intentional on Zhou Guoping's part. Zhou Guoping probably shares an optimistic view on human nature with Marx and some New Left thinkers.* Marx believed that once class confrontation is ended as the result of abolishing private ownership, men will regain their essence as "species beings" and live in constructive relations. In line with Marx, most New Left thinkers viewed man's antisocial and destructive instincts as results of irrational social conditions, not an inherent part of human psyche. On this issue again Zhou Guoping was expressing his own conviction rather than interpreting Nietzsche.

The analysis of the concepts of "master morality" and "slave morality" is a weak spot in the booklet. Instead of relying on Nietzsche's genealogy of

---

* Zhou Guoping often refers to Marx, Adorno, Horkheimer, and Marcuse in his writings.

morals, Zhou Guoping worked out an interpretation of his own which hardly touches the core of Nietzsche's moral philosophy. He explained that, in terms of man's relation with his "self," the "masters" are those who are capable of creating values and live as their own legislator. In contrast, a cowardly, lazy, and irresponsible "slave" can do nothing but follow conventions. In terms of man's relations with other men, the "master morality" emphasizes self-respect, while the "slave morality" relies on "pity." Zhou Guoping added, "Nietzsche did not oppose extending a helping hand to sufferers. In his view, the best help resides in boosting the sufferers' self-respect and their will to change."[28] In terms of man's attitude to life, "slave morality" is characterized by cowardice and hypocrisy; the "master morality" by sincerity. By criticizing "slave morality" and advocating "master morality," Nietzsche intended to "create a wholesome, courageous, independent, enterprising, and sincere type of man," or in Nietzsche's own words, to attain "the highest power and splendor actually possible to the type man."[29]

In the mid-1980s China's publishing industry was still handicapped by an ideological rigidity. An earlier manuscript of *Nietzsche at the Turn of Century* had been turned down by one publisher for its alleged "absence of Marxist viewpoint." Zhou Guoping added a few paragraphs at the end of the seventh chapter when he submitted the book to another publisher that eventually accepted it. To give his book a critical tone he commented that "Nietzsche's aristocratic sentiment undermined nearly all his ideas that were originally rational," and Nietzsche's thought about the two moralities was another case of "revolutionary premises leading to reactionary conclusions."[30] Here the author made an allusion:

> We will have no future if we adopt either an aristocratism that sacrifices equality in favor of progress, or the ideal of the small proprietors that sacrifices progress in exchange for equality. Modern socialism seeks a union of equality and progress, a social ideal that guarantees the full development of the talents of all individuals.[31]

In contemporary China the "ideal of small proprietors" is a phrase often used to characterize Mao Zedong's policy by his Marxist critics. Apparently Zhou Guoping was warning against both jungle capitalism and egalitarianism posed as socialism. The author, however, considered such comments to be irrelevant to a discussion of moral philosophy and he dropped them in the book's later editions.[32]

In the chapter on "The Present and the Future of Mankind," Zhou Guoping treated the concept of superman as a remedy for contemporary civilization. In his view, Nietzsche criticized modern civilization for two reasons: its decadence—the degeneration of the instincts of life, and its philistinism—the poverty of spiritual life. Nietzsche created the "superman" to overcome such a civilization. Zhou Guoping cautiously referred to "superman" as the embodiment of the master morality and as a symbol of a type of man that has not yet been produced. By carefully explicating a passage from *Ecco Homo*, Zhou Guoping showed how the theory of superman differs from both the Darwinian theory of evolution and Carlyle's hero worship.[33]

The ninth chapter, "Poet-Philosopher," seems out of place in an otherwise well-organized book. It reads more like an afterthought than a summary. Its first section, "Aesthetic Life," repeats earlier discussions of the Dionysian and the Apollonian. The second section, "Aesthetic Being," claims that Nietzsche meant to substitute traditional metaphysical systems with an aesthetic ontology. Although supported with quotations from *The Birth of Tragedy* and *The Will to Power*, its frequent reference to the concept of "Being" reveals more of a Heideggerian metaphysical urge than Nietzsche's philosophical drive. In the final section the author argued that since no rational reasoning could reach philosophic truth, Nietzsche was able to convey his ideas only through a poetic language that suggests rather than describes.

Zhou Guoping's second major work on Nietzsche was *Nietzsche and Metaphysics* published in 1991.* According to the book's postscript, the book was "intended to be a scholarly work" and the author was "to treat Nietzsche as a rigorous philosopher and to clarify his thought on the most basic issue, the issue of metaphysics."[34] Zhou Guoping's predilection for metaphysics and for rigorous philosophic system served him well in his earlier work. It gave *Nietzsche at the Turn of the Century* a certain degree of simplicity that is desirable for an introductory book. In the case of a scholarly project, however, his efforts to assign a structure to Nietzsche are sometimes misleading. I am not suggesting that one has to treat Nietzsche piecemeal. There is always the option of grasping Nietzsche's philosophy in

---

* It was originally a dissertation completed in 1988.

its entirety without fitting it into a metaphysical frame, as exemplified by Peter Heller's *Studies on Nietzsche*.*

Unlike his earlier book which draws on several major works by Nietzsche, *Nietzsche and Metaphysics* relies heavily on one book—*The Will to Power*, a collection of Nietzsche's notes edited by his sister Elizabeth Förster-Nietzsche after his death. Even its structure and chapter titles reflect the influence of *The Will to Power*, as shown by the following table:[35]

Chapter titles of *Nietzsche and Metaphysics*	Corresponding section titles of *The Will to Power*
Chapter 1. European Nihilism: Crisis of Metaphysics	Book One. European Nihilism
Chapter 2. Critique of Logic and Language: Psychological Analysis of Metaphysics	Book Three. I. The Will to Power as Knowledge
Chapter 3. Critique of Religion and Morality: Psychological Analysis of Metaphysics II	Book Two. I. Critique of Religion Book Two. II. Critique of Morality
Chapter 4. Perspectivism: a Non-Metaphysical Epistemology	Book Three. I. The Will to Power as Knowledge
Chapter 5. The Will to Power and Eternal Recurrence: Reconstruction or Sublation of Metaphysics	Book Three. III. The Will to Power as Society and Individual Book Four. III. The Eternal Recurrence
Chapter 6. An Aesthetic Defense: Art as a Supplement to Metaphysics	Book Three. IV. The Will to Power as Art

In *Nietzsche at the Turn of the Century*, Zhou Guoping frequently used such expressions as "life in its totality," the "universal life," the "universal

---

* Peter Heller, *Studies on Nietzsche* (Bouvier Verlag Herbert Grundmann: Bonn, 1980)

will," the "world as a whole," or "Being" to explain Nietzsche's philosophical concepts. Although a metaphysical system is implied, the booklet itself can still be appreciated on a non-metaphysical level. In *Nietzsche and Metaphysics* the metaphysical essence of the world is the author's central concern.

Of the four completed chapters, the first three can be viewed as interpretative comments on *The Will to Power*.* The last chapter deserves more attention, for it is the final touch of Zhou Guoping's reconstruction of Nietzsche's metaphysics. The chapter is divided into three parts. In the first part, "The Way to Reconstruct Metaphysics," Zhou Guoping tried to demonstrate that Nietzsche had developed the "principle of analogy"—a complicated theory about how man is capable of accessing the world of "appearance" or "becoming." According to a hypothesis of Nietzsche, an individual's body, understood as a combination of its physiological and psychological functions, contains the memory of the whole process of becoming. Zhou Guoping compared such a concept of "body" with Freud's "Id", and its memory with Jung's "collective unconscious," or "archetypes." Since an "analogy" exists between the individual body and the essence of the world, it is possible for an individual to access "Being," not through rational thinking, but through irrational experience, through the Dionysian.[36]

Based on the "principle of analogy," Zhou Guoping was able to give the concept of the will to power a collectivist or socialist twist in the second part of the fourth chapter. Zhou Guoping treated the "will to power" as an alternative phrase for the "world of appearance." If "becoming" describes the external character of the "world of appearance," explained Zhou Guoping, the "will to power" describes its inner content.[37] Zhou Guoping emphasized that Nietzsche meant by "power" "the inner power, the profusion of life, the transcendence of life, and the self-discipline of the will." Moreover, "power" does not derive from an isolated individual but from the "whole line of mankind that has led to him." Therefore whether an individual has the will to power must be judged by whether he has brought the "total life of mankind" to a course of "ascendance, strength, and exuberance" or a course of "decline, weakness and degeneration."[38] Here again Zhou Guoping had merged Nietzsche with young Marx.

---

* Chapter three and chapter six listed in the above table were planned but not written, see the "Postscript" in *Nietzsche and Metaphysics*, 246.

The next part of the last chapter deals with the idea of "eternal recurrence." In Zhou Guoping's view, "If Nietzsche used the 'will to power' to explain the dynamics of 'becoming,' then the 'eternal recurrence' is a concept he used to explain the pattern of 'becoming.'"[39] The eternal recurrence, according to Zhou Guoping, has three implications. First, the concept has its origin in a metaphysical craving on Nietzsche's part. Having rejected the idea of eternity in a Christian sense or in a traditional metaphysical sense, Nietzsche needed a different kind of "eternity" to impart a meaning to life. As a result Nietzsche invented the "eternal recurrence," that is, "eternity" in the "recurrence."[40] Second, the eternal recurrence is "the heaviest thought" and "the heaviest burden" for Nietzsche. While the eternal recurrence preserves life for eternity, making death no longer an irreversible fact, it also presumes the eternal recurrence of death. From one point of view, the wheel of recurrence seems an infinite repetition of life, from the other, it seems an infinite repetition of death. More important, in the grinding wheel of the eternal recurrence, there is no room left for creation, "This radical fatalism leads to radical nihilism, since it pronounces meaninglessness to be eternal."[41] Third, the eternal recurrence imposes a moral imperative on man and forces him to ask himself, "Are you willing to repeat your life as it is an infinite number of times?" Man has to assume responsibility for his own actions in his life, since what waits for him is not the one-time last judgment, but numerous judgments in the form of recurrences of his life. In the idea of *"amor fai,"* explained Zhou Guoping, Nietzsche was able to combine a life-affirming attitude and a recognition of man's responsibility for his will and action.[42]

Zhou Guoping was aware of theoretical difficulties in his interpretation. He concluded the chapter with an ingenious proposition that is less optimistic:

> As long as eternal recurrence is the repetition of all details with no exception, the freedom for revaluation of values will be groundless. . . . In order to reconcile the theory of eternal recurrence with Nietzsche's other theories, such as the will to power, the revaluation of all values, and the superman, one must consider the repetition of details to be Nietzsche's delusion. . . . Thus in terms of cosmology, the eternal recurrence should be viewed as Nietzsche's description of the never ceasing will to power; ethically it is an affirmation of the inexhaustible total life. An eternal recurrence that allows changes of details leaves room for man's freedom, since from the viewpoint of the infinite universe of becoming, is it not true that man's freedom resides only in changing details?[43]

According to the author's original plan, *Nietzsche and Metaphysics* should have six chapters instead of four.[44] He had probably abandoned one of the two chapters for political reasons. Its subject—"A Critique of Religion and Morality" includes topics that are too inconvenient for a dissertation. The other unwritten chapter, "An Aesthetic Defense: Art as Supplement to Metaphysics," was probably given up for a theoretical dilemma. If Zhou Guoping were to write such a chapter, he would either have to deal with the mere concept of art or write a poem instead of a book chapter. Moreover, such a chapter would have been easily turned into its opposite: "An Aesthetic Refutation: Art as a Substitute for Metaphysics," thereby nullifying much of what the author has written. It seems that Zhou Guoping was projecting his own dilemma on Nietzsche when, at the end of his book, he referred to a Nietzsche torn "between criticizing metaphysics and reconstructing metaphysics."[45]

In the book's postscript dated June 1989, Zhou Guoping told readers that he was going to "part with Nietzsche... for a very long time, if not forever," for "one tends to get tired after working on a historical figure for too long a time."[46] There may be another reason he did not mention. While Zhou Guoping was discussing Nietzsche on a philosophical level, many others, especially the young, were eager to play with Nietzschean ideas as if they were political pronouncements. Some saw Nietzsche as a champion for a highly individualistic philosophy and used him to criticize the CCP's collectivist tendency; others found in him the rationale for an outright rejection of China's political and cultural heritage; still others used the Dionysian as a metaphor for a revolutionary uprising against the establishment. In the 1989 mass movement for more democracy, some of these young Nietzschean figures played a prominent role. It is not surprising that official newspapers held Nietzsche, among others, responsible for the movement. It seems that Zhou Guoping intended to distance himself from the much politicized Nietzsche. After a major setback in 1989, the process of gradual democratization resumed in China, so did the study of Western philosophy. In the 1990s Chinese scholars continued to translate, study and discuss Nietzsche, but Zhou Guoping, Nietzsche's most brilliant interpreter in China, so far has remained aloof.

A whole century has passed since Chinese intellectuals began to study Western ideas. After much hard work and suffering, often under impossible conditions, Chinese students of Western ideas have come of age. Their efforts in appropriating Western ideas and reassessing China's own intellectual heritage are beginning to bear fruit in the emergence of a more dynamic and humane society. With that prospect in mind, the current book should be viewed only as the prehistory of a more profound synthesis of ideas Western and Eastern in the coming century.

Notes

1. Friedrich Nietzsche, *Thus Spoke Zarathustra*, [查拉斯圖拉如是說] trans. Gao Han (Chu Tunan), Shanghai: Jiaotong Books, 1952 (Originally published in 1947).
2. The few final volumes of *Complete Works of Marx and Engels* were completed in the 1980s. While the works of Lenin and Stalin had also been translated, their influence on Chinese intellectuals was much smaller than that of Marx and Engels.
3. For example, see Mu Gong, "Nietzsche," *Yunnan Daily*, May 15, 1982 [木公，尼采] and Heifeng, "Nietzsche—the Forefather of Fascism," *Workers' Daily*, May 5, 1984 [海丰，法西斯思想的鼻祖]
4. Le Daiyun, "Nietzsche and Contemporary Literature," *Beijing University Journal* (Philosophy), no. 3, (1980); Zhao Xiuyi, "Nietzsche's Superman and his Superman Philosophy" in *Eastern China Normal School Journal* [《華東師大學報》(哲學版)], no. 2, (1983), 30-33, 36; and Qian Bixian, "Lu Xun and the Philosophy of Nietzsche," *Chinese Social Science* [《中國社會科學》], 1982, no. 3, 113-130.
5. Ru Xin, "On the Origin of Nietzsche's Theory of Tragedy," *Foreign Aesthetics*, series 1, (Beijing, Commercial Press, 1985).
6. Zhang Rulun, "A misunderstood philosopher—my views on Nietzsche's philosophy," *Book Forest* [《書林》], no. 3, May 1985. The same article was published in digest in a national newspaper, *Newsletter of Theoretical Discussions* [《理論信息報》], August 26, 1985.
7. George Brandes, *Friedrich Nietzsche*, trans. by An Yanming (Beijing: Workers' Press, 1985). The book was based on the English translation by A. G. Chater (London: W. Heinemann, 1914).
8. Zhou Guoping, *You Have Only One Life* [《只有一個人生》] (Wuhan: Hubei People Press, 1991), 101-103.
9. His writing on Marxist humanism could not be published after the Campaign against Spiritual Pollution. See *ibid.*, 80.
10. *Ibid.*, 252.
11. Zhou Guoping, *Only One Life*, 100-101.
12. *Ibid.*, 83.
13. Zhou Guoping, *Nietzsche at the Turning Point of the Century* (Shanghai: Shanghai People's Press, 1986), 251-52.
14. Zhou Guoping, *At the Turn of the Century*, 30.

[15] *Ibid.*, 61.
[16] *Ibid.*, 70-71.
[17] *Ibid.*, 77.
[18] *Ibid.*, 82.
[19] *Ibid.*, 90-91.
[20] *Ibid.*, 96-97.
[21] *Ibid.*, 123-131. Nietzsche discussed the concept of "health selfishness" in *Thus Spoke Zarathustra*, see *Portable Nietzsche*, 302.
[22] *Ibid.*, p. 144. The English translation is from Friedrich Nietzsche, *The Gay Science*, trans. by Walter Kaufmann (New York: Vintage Books, A Division of Random House, 1974), 73-74.
[23] *Ibid.*
[24] Nietzsche, *Gay Science*, 73.
[25] Zhou Guoping, *At the Turn of the Century*, 178-179.
[26] *Ibid.*, 184.
[27] Nietzsche, *Twilight of the Idols*, from *Portable Nietzsche*, 487.
[28] Zhou Guoping, *At the Turn of the Century*, 190.
[29] *Ibid.*, 196. The quoted words are based on *Genealogy of Morals*, see *Basic Writings*, 456.
[30] *Ibid.*, 197.
[31] *Ibid.*, 198.
[32] See the book's Taipei edition (1992) and the 1997 reprint.
[33] Zhou Guoping, *At the Turn of the Century*, 219.
[34] Zhou Guoping, *Nietzsche and Metaphysics* (Hunan Education Press, 1990), 243.
[35] The table is based on Zhou Guoping's book and *The Will to Power*, translated by Walter Kaufmann and R. J. Hollingdale (New York: Vintage Books, 1968).
[36] *Ibid.*, 188-190.
[37] *Ibid.*, 216.
[38] *Ibid.*, 201-203.
[39] *Ibid.*, 220.
[40] *Ibid.*, 226
[41] *Ibid.*, 232.
[42] *Ibid.*, 234.
[43] *Ibid.*, 235-236.
[44] *Ibid.*, 246-247.
[45] *Ibid.*, 243.
[46] *Ibid.*, 246.

Selected Bibliography

Beijing Normal University, Dept. of Chinese Literature. *Sources of Contemporary Literature*, [北京師範大學中文系，《中國現代文學史參考資料》] Vol. 1, Part II. Beijing: Beijing Normal University Press, 1959.

Beijing University, Dept. of Philosophy, *Selected Sources of History of Philosophy of Contemporary China* [《中國現代哲學史教學資料選集》]. Beijing: Beijing University Press, 1988.

Bonner, Joey. *Wang Kuo-wei: an Intellectual History* Cambridge. Mass: Harvard University Press, 1986.

Cai Yuanpei. *Selected Works of Cai Yuanpei* [《蔡元培選集》，北京人民出版社，1984] Beijing: People Press, 1984.

———. *Political Writings of Cai Yuanpei*. [《蔡元培政治論著》] Hebei: Hebei People Press, 1985.

———. "The European War and Philosophy," in *Political Works of Cai Yuanpei*. Ed. Gao Shuping, Hebei Renmin Press, 1985. pp. 167-172. [" 歐戰與哲學 "爲蔡元培在北大 " 國際研究 " 演講會上的演說辭，發表于《新青年》五卷五號（October 1918）和《東方雜誌》十六卷一號（January 1919.）高叔平編，《蔡元培政治論著》，河北人民出版社，1985.

Chang, Hao. *Liang Ch'i-chao and Intellectual Transition in China, 1890–1907*. Cambridge, Massachusetts: Harvard University Press, 1971.

Chen Duxiu. *Selected Writings of Chen Duxiu*. [北京，三聯書店，《陳獨秀文章選編》] Beijing: Sanlian Books, 1984.

———. *Autobiography of Chen Duxiu*. [《陳獨秀自傳》，包括《陳獨秀自述》及《陳獨秀最後論文和書信》], Hong Kong, Xiandai Press, 1969.

Chen Quan. *Questioning the Heaven*. [《天問》] Jiangsu Wenyi Press, 1985. (The book was originally published in 1928.)

———. "From Schopenhauer to Nietzsche," [《從叔本華到尼采》] *Tsinghuan Journal* [《清華學報》] vol. 11, no. 2, (April, 1936)

———. "Nietzsche and Modern Historical Education," [尼采與近代歷史教育] in *Quarterly of Yet-sen Association of Culture and Education* [中山文化教育館季刊], Fall, 1937.

———. *Blue Butterflies*. [《藍蝴蝶》] Shanghai: Commercial Press, 1940.

———. *The Mansion of Golden Crane*. [《黃鶴樓》] Chongqing: Commercail Press, 1945.

———. *Wild Rose*. [《野玫瑰》] Chongqing: Commercial Press, 1942. Originally published in *Journal of Humanities*, [文史雜誌] vol. 1, no. 6–8 (June 16 to July 17, 1941).

———. *The Golden Ring* [金指環] in *Military Affairs and Politics*, [《軍事與政治》] vol. 2, no. 5 and no. 6, vol. 3. no. 1 (from April to June, 1942).

Chen Wanxiong. *Chen Duxiu Before the New Cultural Movement, 1879–1915*. [陳萬雄,《新文化運動前的陳獨秀,一八七九至一九一九》] Hong Kong: Hong Kong Chinese University Press, 1979.

Cheung, Chiu-yee. *Nietzsche and the Development of Lu Xun's Thought*. [尼采與魯迅思想發展] Hongkong: Qing Wen Bookstore, 1987.

———. *Nietzsche in China (1904–1992): An Annotated Bibliography*. Canberra, Australia: Australian National University Press, 1992..

Ding Wenjiang and Zhao Fengtian. *The Life of Liang Qichao: Selected Sources in Chronological Order*. Shanghai: People Press, 1983. [丁文江,趙丰田,《梁任公先生年譜長篇》,上海人民出版社,1983.]

Feigon, Lee. *Chen Duxiu: Founder of the Chinese Communist Party*. Princeton, New Jersey: Princeton University Press, 1983.

Fung Yu-lan. *A Short History of Chinese Philosophy*. Trans. by Derk Bodde. New York: The Free Press, A Division of Macmillan Publishing Co., 1966.

Gálik, Von Marián. "Nietzsche in China (1918–1925)." *Nachrichten der Gesellschaft für Natur und Völkerkunde Ostasiens*, vol. 110 (1971): 5–48.

Gao Jucun; Chen Feng; Tang Zhennan and Tian Yuliang. *Young Mao Zedong*. Beijing: Publisher for Historical Sources of the Chinese Communist Party, 1990. [高菊村,陳峰,唐振南,田余糧,《青年毛澤東》北京:中共黨史資料出版社]

Gong Jimin and Fang Rennian. *A Biography of Guo Moruo* [龔濟民,方仁年,《郭沫若年譜》]. Tianjin: Tianjin People's Press, 1982.

Guo Moruo. *Goddes*. [女神] Shanghai: Taidong Book, 1921.

———. *Works of Guo Moruo* [《沫若文集》]. 12 vols. Beijing: People's Literature Press, 1959.

———. *Complete Works of Guo Moruo*. Literature Series [《郭沫若全集》文學編]. Beijing: People's Literature Press, 1982.

Grasso, June; Jay Corrin & Michael Kort, *Modernization and Revolution in China*. New York: 1997 (Revised Edition).

Heller, Peter. *Studies on Nietzsche*. Bonn: Bouvier, 1980.

Hsia Tsi-an, *The Gate of Darkness*. Seattle: University of Washington Press, 1968.

Hu Shi. *Writings of Hu Shi*. [《胡適文存》] 4 vols. Shanghai: Ya Dong Tu Shu Guan, 1930.

Huang, Philip C. *Liang Ch'i-ch'ao and Modern Chinese Liberalism.* Seattle and London: University of Washington Press, 1972.

Ito Toramaru. *Lu Xun and Eschatology* [《魯迅と終末論》]. Tokyo: 龍溪書店, 1975.

———. *Lu Xun and the Japanese: the Modernity of Asia and the Concept of "Individuality"* [《魯迅と日本人，アジアの近代と「個」の思想》]. Tokyo: Asahi Shinbon Press, 1983.

———. "Early Lu Xun's View of Western Culture-Japan's Nietzsche and Lu Xun's Nietzsche (an Outline)" [伊藤虎丸，"早期魯迅的西方文化觀（提綱）] in *Trends in Lu Xun Studies* (monthly) [《魯迅研究動態》] 1986, no. 11, p.34.

Jia Zhifang. *Literary Associations and Schools of Contemporary China* [南京：江蘇教育出版社，《中國現代文學社團流派》]. Nanjing: Jiansu Education Press, 1989.

Jian Bozan. "Idealism in Historical Science and its Critique," in *Quarterly of Yet-sen Association of Culture and Education* [中山文化教育館季刊], Fall, 1937.

Kang Youwei. *Ta T'ung Shu. The One-World Philosophy of K'ang Yu-wei,* trans. by Laurence G. Thompson. London: Allen & Unwin, 1958.

Kidd, Benjamin, *Principles of Western Civilisation.* London: MacMillan and Co. Limited, 1902.

———. *Social Evolution.* Chicago: Charles H. Sergel Company, 1894.

Le Daiyun. "Nietzsche and Contemporary Literature in China." *Beijing University Journal* no. 3 (June, 1980): 20–33.

Levenson, Joseph R. *Liang Ch'i-ch'ao and the Mind of Modern China.* London: Cambridge University Press, 1967.

Li Dazhao. *Selected Writings of Li Dazhao.* [《李大釗文選》] Beijing: People's Press, 1984.

Li Rui, *Comrade Mao Zedong's Early Revolutionary Activities.* [李銳，《毛澤東同志的初期革命活動》] 北京：人民出版社] Beijing: Chinese Youth Press, 1957.

Li Shicen. *A Brief Introduction to Superman Philosophy.* [《超人哲學淺說》] Shanghai: Commercial Press, 1931.

———. *Essays of Li Shicen.* [《李石岑論文集》] Shanghai: Commercial Press, 1924.

———. *Lectures of Li Shicen.* [《李石岑演講集》] Shanghai: Commercial Press, 1924.

Liang Qichao. *Collected Works of Liang Qichao.* [《飲冰室文集》] 16 vols. Edited by Zhijun Lin. Taipei: Zhonghuo Shuju, 1960.

———. *Liang Qichao's Works by Categories* [《飲冰室類編》] 2 vols. Taipei: Huazheng Books, 1974.

―――. *Recent Works of Liang Qichao (vol. 1).* [《梁任公近著》] Taipei: Wenhai Press, 1978 (originally published in 1922).

―――, ed. *General Observation and Reflections on the Journey to Europe.* Shanghai: Commercial Press, 1922.

Lu Xun. *Complete Works of Lu Xun* [《鲁迅全集》]. 16 vols. Beijing: Renmin Wenxue, 1981.

―――. *Diary of a Madman and Other Stories.* Trans. by William A. Lyell. Honolulu: University of Hawaii Press, 1990.

―――. *Selected Works.* Trans. by Xianyi Yang and Gladys Yang. 4 vols. Beijing: Foreign Languages Press, 1956.

―――. *Thirty Years' Writings by Lu Xun.* [《鲁迅三十年集》] 8 vols. Hong Kong: Xinyi Chuban She, 1971.

Lundberg, Lennart. *Lu Xun As a Translator: Lu Xun's Translation and Introduction of Literatury Theory, 1903-1936.* Föreningen För Orientaliska Studier 23. Stockholm: Orientaliska Studier Stockholom University, 1989.

Mao Zedong. *Colleted Writings of Mao Zedong* [《毛澤東集》]. 10 vols. Tokyo: Sososha, 1972.

―――. *Supplement to Collected Writings of Mao Zedong* [《毛澤東集補集》]. 10 vols. Tokyo: Sososha, 1983.

Masaaki Kosaka, ed. *Japanese Thought in the Meiji Era.* Translated and adopted by David Abosch. Tokyo: Pan-Pacific Press, 1958.

Museum of the Chinese Revolution and the Museum of Hunan, ed. *Sources of the People's Renovation* [《新民學會資料》]. Beijing: People's Press, 1980.

Nietzsche, Friedrich. *Basic Writings of Nietzsche.* Translated by Walter Kaufmann. New York: Random House, 1968.

―――. *The Portable Nietzsche.* Translated by Walter Kaufmann. New York: Penguin Books, 1976.

―――. *Daybreak: Thoughts on the Prejudices of Morality.* Translated by R.J. Hollingdale. Cambridge and New York: Cambridge University Press, 1982.

―――. *Human, All Too Human: A Book for Free Spirit.* Translated by R. J. Hollingdale. Cambridge and New York: Cambridge University Press, 1986.

―――. *The Gay Science.* Translated by Walter Kaufmann. New York: Vintage Books, A Division of Random House, 1974.

―――. *The Will to Power.* Translated by Walter Kaufmann and R. J. Hollingdale. New York: Vintage Books, A Division of Random House, 1968.

―――. *Untimely Meditations.* Translated by R.J. Hollingdale. Cambridge and New York: Cambridge University Press, 1983.

Onoe Kanehide. "Lu Xun and Nietzsche." [尾上兼英，魯迅と尼采] *Journal of the Japanese Society of Chinese Studies* [日本中國學會報] no. 13, (1961): 102–115.

Parkes, Graham, ed. *Nietzsche and Asian thought*. Chicago and London: University of Chicago Press, 1991.

Paulsen, Friedrich. *System der Ethik mit einem Umriss der Staats und Gesellschaftslehre*. Berlin: Hertz, 1889.

———. *A System of Ethics*. Trans. by Frank Thilly. New York: Scribner's Sons, 1899.

Pusey, James Reeve. *China and Charles Darwin*. Cambridge, Mass: Harvard University Press, 1983.

Quarterly of the Sun Yet-sen Institute of Culture and Education [中山文化教育館季刊], Fall 1937.

Rosenthal, Bernice Glatzer, ed. *Nietzsche in Russia*. Princton, NJ: Princeton Un. Press, 1986.

———, ed. *Nietzsche and Soviet Culture: Ally and Adversary*. Cambridge University Press, 1994.

Roy, David Tod. *Kuo Mo-Jo: The Early Years*. Harvard Eastern Asian Series No. 55. Cambridge, Massachusetts: Harvard University Press, 1971.

Schram, Stuart R. *The Political Thoguht of Mao Tse–tung*. New York: Praegue, 1969.

———, ed. *Mao's Road to Power: Revolutionary Writings 1912–1949*. New York: Columbia University Press, 1992.

Schwartz, Benjamin. *In Search of Wealth and Power—Yen Fu and the West*. Cambridge, Massachusetts: Belknap Press of Harvard University Press, 1964.

Shiga Masatoshi, "A Study of Lu Xun's Translation," [志賀正年，魯迅翻譯研究] in *Tenri Univerity Journal* [天理大學學報] no. 15 (1955): 71–92.

Spence, Jonathan D. *The Search for Modern China*. New York: W. W. Norton, 1990.

Siao Yu. *Mao Tse-tung and I were Beggers*. Syracuse University, 1959.

Su Guangwen. *Selected Sources of Literary Theories*. [《文學理論史料選》] Chengdu: Sichuan Education Press, 1988.

Wang Guowei. *Complete Works of Wang Guowei* [《王觀堂先生全集》] 16 vols. Taipei: Wenhua Press, 1968.

Wang Xiaobo; Li Rizhang; Li Rongzhong. eds. *Kang Youwei and Liang Qichao*. Modern Chinese Thinkers Series, No. 3. Taipei: Giant Press, 1978. [王曉波，李日章，李容中等編，《現代中國思想家》第三集《康有爲，梁起超》，台北，巨人出版社，1978.]

Warrring States. [《戰國策》] (A journal published in Kunmin from April 1940 to early 1941.)

Windelband, Wilhelm W. *A History of Philosophy*. Authorized trans. by James H. Tufts. New York: the Macmillan Company, 1914. (Reprint of 1901 based on the second German Edition)

Yan Fu. *Selected Essays and Poems of Yan Fu*. Selected and annotated by Zhou Zhenpu. Beijing, People's Literature Press, 1959.

Yi Jianfei and Fang Songhua, eds. *Selected Readings of Contemporary Chinese Philosophy*. [惲劍飛，方忪華，《中國現代哲學原著選》] Shanghai: Fudan University Press, 1989.

Zhao Jiabi, ed. *Grand Series of the Chinese New Literature*. [趙家璧編，《中國新文學大系》] Shanghai: Liangyou Tushu Gongsi, 1936.

Zhongguo Geming Bowuguan and Hunan Sheng Bowuguan, eds. *Sources of the Study Society of People's Renovation*. [中國革命博物館，湖南博物館，《新民學會資料》] Beijing: People's Press, 1980.

Zhou Guoping. *Nietzsche at the Turn of the Century*. [上海人民出版社，《尼采在世紀的轉折點上》] Shanghai: Shanghai People's Press, 1986 (reprinted in 1997).

———. *Nietzsche at the Turn of the Century*. [臺北，錦德圖書有限公司，《尼采在世紀的轉折點上》] Taipei: Jin De Books Limited, 1992.

———. *Nietzsche and Metaphysics*. [《尼采與形而上學》] Hunan Education Press, 1990.

———. *You Have Only One Life* [《只有一個人生》]. Wuhan: Hubei People Press, 1991.

Zhou Xiashou. *People and Events in Lu Xun's Early Life* [《魯迅的故家》]. Shanghai: Shanghai Chuban Gongsi, 1953.

Index

Adorno, Theodor, 125
anarchism
    anarchists in China, 63
Andreyev, Leonid, 48, 56
anti-Semitism, 59
Artysbashev, Mikhail, 58, 59, 60, 67, 70
Austria, 81

Bentham, Jeremy, 9
Bergson, Henri, 91
Bismarck, Otto von, 80
Bolshevik Revolution, 33, 35, 64, 66, 83
Book of Rites, 4
Brandes, George, 118
Buddhism, 6, 31
Byron, George Gordon, 51

Cai Yuanpei, 82, 84
capitalism, 126
CCP. *See* Communist Party, Chinese
Chekhov, Anton, 48
Chen Duxiu, 41, 54, 135, 136
    see Chapter 3, 29–34
Chen Quan. *See Chaper 7*
Chiang Kai-shek, 66, 69, 107
China
    1911 Revolution, 24, 29, 54, 65
    civil war (1946-1949), 115
    compared with the West, 31
    culture policy between 1949-1978, 115–16
    culture policy since 1979, 118, 126, 131
    Great Proletarian Cultural Revolution, 88
    Incident (March 18, 1926), 63
    Incident (May 30, 1925), 62
    intellectuals in the PRC, 116
    Marxism promoted in the PRC, 115, 116
    Marxist studies in the PRC, 117
    May Fourth protests in 1919, 61
    modern Chinese language, 117–18
    New Marxist Movement in early 1980s, 119
    student movement for more democracy, (March to June, 1989), 131
    translations of Western philosophical works in the PRC, 116
    use of vernacular Chinese in writing, 41
Chinese Academy of Social Sciences, 118, 119
    its predecessor, 116
Christianity, 31, 33, 53, 97, 130
    missionary publication in China, 9
Chu Tunan, 115
Comintern, 34, 63, 72, 73, 87
Communist Party, Chinese, 34, 36, 62, 63, 65, 66, 71, 72, 73, 86, 87, 88, 107, 109, 117, 131
    founding of, 34, 36
Confucius
    as thinker of future generation, 4, 9
    Confucianism criticized, 30, 31, 56, 95, 97
    principle of extending, 32
Copernicus, Nicolaus, 36
Czech literature, 47
Czechoslovakia, 81

Darwin, Charles, 6, 36

Deng Xiaoping, 118
Descartes, René, 119
Dewey, John, 91
Don Quixote, 68

Eckhart, Meister, 18
egalitarianism, 126
Engels, Friedrich, 40
 translation of his works in the PRC, 117
England
 Chinese students in, 6
 English literature, 51
Enlightenment, 85, 86
Eurocommunism, 119
Evolution
 ethical evolution, 52
 ethical evolution, Lu Xun, 57

Fadeyev, Aleksandr Aleksandrovich, 72
 and Lu Xun, 69–70
Feigon, Lee, 42
fellow traveler, 67
feminist movement, 9
Feng Xuefeng, 71, 72, 73
Feuerbach, Ludwig Andreas, 116
Fichte, Johann Gottlieb, 80, 82, 110
Finland
 Finnish literature, 47
Förster-Nietzsche, Elizabeth, 128
France, 33
Freud, Sigmund, 129
Fujino, 46–47
Fujita Toyohachi, 17

Galton, Francis, 40
Germany
 German militarism, 31
 in WWII, 110
 Nazi persecution of Jews, 101
 Nazi seizure of power, 101
Gogol, Nikolai, 48, 56

Gorky
 Maxim, 66
Guo Moruo, 41, 67
 See Chapter 3, 36–40

Haeckel
 Ernst Heinrich, 48
Hartmann
 Eduard von, 109
Hegel, G. W. F., 110, 116
Heidegger, Martin, 127
Heller, Peter, 128
Hitler, Adolf, 101, 110
Hong Kong, 5
Horkheimer, Max, 125
Hu Shih, 41
 See Chapter 3, 40–41
Hugo, Victor, 30
Hume, David, 119
Hundred Days Reform, 8, 10, 46
Hungary, 81
 Hungarian literature, 47, 51
Husserl, Edmund, 91
Huxley, Thomas Henry, 6

Ibsen, Henrik, 49
individualism
 versus nationalism, 7, 10
Ito Toramaru, 74, 75

James, William, 91
Japan
 Chinese students in, 34, 36, 46
 Japanese translation of Soviet literature, 66
Jhering, Rudolf von, 8
Jhering, Rudolf von, 8
Jian Bozen, 107
Jung, Karl Gustav, 129

Kang Youwei, 4, 5, 6, 8, 9, 52

Index

and Buddhism, 5
background and main ideas, 4–5
in Hong Kong, 5
life and ideas, 4–5
three stages of history, 4
Kano Naoki, 25
Kant, Immanuel, 9, 15, 17, 20, 22, 23, 31, 102
Kato Hiroyuki, 8
Kawakami Hajime, 39, 40
Kidd, Benjamin, 1, 2, 3, 9, 10, 80, 81, 82, 83
on Nietzsche and Marx, 3
Kierkegaard, Sören, 12, 49, 91
Korea
nationalist movement, 80
Krasinski, Zygmunt, 51
Kropotkin, Peter, 82

labor movement, 9
League of Left-wing Writers, 72
Lenin, Nikolai, 39, 40, 107
Lermontov, Mikhail, 51
Li Dazhao, 41
see Chapter 3, 34–36
Li Shicen. See Chapter 6
Liang Qichao, 83. See Chapter 1
"People's Renovation", *1, 8, 10*
and Kang Youwei, 4–5
early education, 4
Lie Zi (a Chinese classic), 22
Lin Shuang, 82
Lin Tongji, 110
Long March, 72
Lu Xiangshan, 120
Lu Xun. See Chapter 4
and Mao Zedong, 72–73
Lunacharsky, Anatoly Vasilyevich
and Lu Xun, 66–69
Lundberg, Lennart, 66
Luo Zhenyu, 24, 25

Mao Zedong, 11, 72, 73, 116, 117. *See Chapter 5*
and Li Shicen, 91
and Lu Xun, 72–73
Marcuse, Herbert, 125
Marx, Karl, 1, 2, 3, 10, 36, 39, 40, 58, 68, 81, 107
"species being", 125
Economic and Philosophical Manuscripts of 1844, 125
translation of his works in the PRC, 117
May Fourth protests in 1919, 61
Mickiewicz, Adam, 51
Mo Di, 31, 32
Moltke, Helmuth Karl von, 80

nationalism
and "national imperialism", 10
criticized, 7
introduced to China, 7
Nationalist Party (GMD), 34, 62, 63, 65, 109
Neruda, Jan, 47
New Culture Movement, 54
New Left, 119, 125
New Youth, 29, 41, 55, 56
Nietzsche
his death, 1
Nietzsche, Friedrich
"becoming hard", 97
"freedom of will" and freedom in "universal will", 123
"go under", 60
"healthy selfishness", 123–24
"Night Song", 71
"preachers of death", 71
"principle of analogy", 129
"self", 123–24
"Untergehen", 60
aestecism and Marxism, 68
amor fati, 122, 130
and Arthur Schopenhauer, 19, 21, 122
and Bolshevik heroes, 69–70

and Bolshevism, 71
and Friedrich Paulsen, 84–86
and Karl Marx, 1, 3, 40, 58, 97–98, 121, 124–25
and Max Stirner, 95–96
and reason, 124
and state, 111
and World War I, 82
aphorisms, 39
Apollonian, 96, 103
Art, Li Shicen, 96
as corrosive influence, 24
as representing the bourgeoisie and petty bourgeoisie, 118
as symbol of individualism, 31
as symptom of the Enlightenment, 85
ascetic ideals, 85
biography, 34
Chinese translation of, 37, 55, 101, 115, 120
Christianity, 97, 125
conscience, 104–5
criticized in the era of Mao Zedong, 115
democracy, 49
Dionysian, 118, 121, 131
Dionysian art, 96
Dionysian art and the "voice of heart", 49–50
Dionysian, will to power, and eternal recurrence considered together, 121–22
elitism criticized, 126
elitism, a populist interpretation, 95
eternal recurrence, 94, 122, 130
forgetfulness, 108
freedom, 122–23
Genealogy of Morals, 51
go under, Untergehen, 60
his philosophy is true but cannot be loved, 23
his rehabilitation in China since 1979, 118
historical sense, 108
Human, All Too Human, 104

iconoclasm, 84–86, 85, 88
imperialism, 12
individual will and universal will, 123
individualism, 49, 95–96, 95–96
instincts, different kinds of, 125
last man, 70, 71
life affirming understood as cruelty, 112
man's nature, 122–23
master morality and slave morality, 30, 31, 35, 63, 96, 125–26
new valuation for man's freedom, 123
nihilism, 84
origin of his metaphysics, 20
pessimism, 104
pity, 97, 126
rationalism and irrationalism, 124–25
responsibilities, 104–5
revaluatioln of all values, 85
revaluation of all values, 41, 125
science, 104
science and art, 104–5
self, two layers of, 123
slave morality, 12
spirit's three metamorphoses, 19, 97, 123
superman, 31, 36, 38, 53, 56, 70, 93, 111, 127
The Birth of Tragedy, 96, 102, 103, 127
The Gay Science, 105, 124
the Will to Power, 19, 127, 128
Thus Spake Zarathustra, influence on Lu Xun, 57
Thus Spoke Zarathustra, 19, 37, 38, 39, 50, 51, 55, 60, 61, 71, 92, 97, 116, 124
tragic hero, 51
Twilight of Idols, 125
Untergehen, 60
Untimely Meditations, 31, 102, 107
will to power, 51, 92, 93, 111, 121–22, 129
will to power and Byron's poem, 51

will to power and social Darwinism, 121
will to power and will to life, 121
will to power as cruelty, 105
will to power as revolutionary will, Lunacharsky, 68
will to power as will to rule and exploit, Lunacharsky, 68
will to power compared with Schopenhauer's will to life, 23
will to power, Chinese word for, 121
World War One, 12
Northern Expedition, 38, 65

Päivärinta, Pietari, 47
Paris Peace Conference, 33, 61
Paulsen, Friedrich, 80, 81, 84
    Chinese translation of *System of Ethics*, 84–86
Payne, Robert, 64
Petöfi, Sandor, 48, 51
Pilnyak, Boris, 64, 65, 66
Plekhanov, Georgy, 107
Poland
    Polish literature, 47, 51
progress, the idea of, 94
Pushkin, Alexander, 51

Qian Xiantong, 55
Qu Qiubai, 67, 71

Red Army, Chinese, 73, 87
reverse social Darwinism, 6, 9
Rosenthal, Bernice Glatzer, 68
Ru Xin, 118
Russell, Bertrand, 40, 79, 91
Russia, 33, 64, 81
    Russian literature, 51
    the Civil War (1918-1920), 69
Russo-Japanese War, 47

Sartre, Jean-Paul, 79
Schopenhauer, Arthur, 16, 17, 18, 19, 20, 21, 22, 23, 24, 35, 49, 85, 102, 103, 104, 105, 106, 107, 121, 122, 135
self-determination, 80
Shelley, Percy Bysshe, 51
Sienkiewicz, Henryk, 47
Sino-Japanese War, the First, 16
Sino-Japanese War, the Second, 72
Six Classics, 120
Slowacki, Juliusz, 51
Smith, Adam, 6
social Darwinism, 6, 7, 8, 31, 32, 52. *Also see* reverse social Darwinism
and reverse social Darwinism, 6
socialism, 126
Spencer, Herbert, 6
Spengler, Oswald, 110
Stirner, Max, 12, 49, 95
Stowe, Harriet Beecher, 46
Su Manshu, 30

Taoka Sayoji, 17
Thilly, Frank, 84
Thus Spake Zarathustra, 73
Tolstoi, Leo, 31, 34, 35, 52, 59, 60, 67, 82
Trotsky, Leon, 40

United Front, the First (1923-1927), 62
United Front, the Second, 72, 73
United Nations
    as a fictional world organization, 11
United States, 33, 101
utopian socialism, 8, 116

Versailles Treaty (1919), 80
Vrchlicky, Jaroslav, 47

Wang Guowei. *See Chapter 2*

Whompoa Military Academy, 65
William II, 80
World War I, 32, 82

Xu Guangping, 63
Xu Guanping, 63

Yan Fu, 6, 8, 52
    reverse social Darwinism, 6

Yanan, 72
Yang Zhu, 32

Zhang Zhidong, 15
Zhou Guoping. *See Chapter 8*
Zhou Yang, 71, 72, 73, 119
Zhu De, 87
Zhuang Zi, 73
Zionism, 80

Literature and the Sciences of Man

This interdisciplinary series is predicated on the conviction that the inevitable development toward increasing specialization requires as its correlative a movement toward integration between the humanities, social sciences, and natural sciences. Titles in the series will deal with "multi-disciplinary" figures, as well as with movements affecting a variety of disciplines. The series editor will also consider manuscripts dealing with methods and strategies in the domains of aesthetic creation, the arts of criticism, and scientific exploration.

Please direct all inquiries to the series editor.

> Peter Heller
> Dept. of Modern Languages & Literatures
> SUNY-Buffalo
> Buffalo, NY 14260